Teaching Written Response to Text

Constructing Quality Answers to Open-ended Comprehension Questions

Nancy N. Boyles

Second Edition

Teaching Written Response to Text
Constructing Quality Answers to Open-ended Comprehension Questions

© 2002 Nancy N. Boyles
All Rights Reserved

Cover Design: Maria Messenger
Layout Design: Billie J. Hermansen

Library of Congress Cataloging-in-Publication Data

Boyles, Nancy N.
    Teaching written response to text : constructing quality answers to open-ended
  comprehension questions / Nancy Boyles
        p. cm.
    Includes bibliographical references and index.
    ISBN 0-929895-50-9
      1. English language—Composition and exercises—Study and teaching (Elementary) 2.
  English language—Composition and exercises—Examinations. I. title

  LB1576 .B55 2001
  372.62'3—dc21

                                                          2001041007

ISBN-10: 0-929895-50-9
ISBN-13: 978-0-929895-50-5

Maupin House Publishing, Inc.
2416 NW 71st Place
Gainesville, FL 32653

1-800-524-0634 / 352-373-5588
352-373-5546 (fax)
www.maupinhouse.com
info@maupinhouse.com

Publishing Professional Resources that Improve Classroom Performance

10 9 8 7 6 5

Dedication

For Ron, husband extraordinaire —
Now *you* can have a turn at the computer.
And Caitlin, forever my lovebug —
You make it (almost) fun
to be the parent of a teenager!

I hear and I forget.

I see and I remember.

I do and I understand.

— Confucius

Table of Contents

    A. According to this text, [who / when / where / why / how] _____? Why is this important?

    B. Choose one word that best describes [name of character / person] and provide evidence from the text to support your choice

    C. What is the problem or conflict in this text? Give specific details to support your answer

    D. Briefly summarize what happens in this story

    E. How does [the main character / important person] solve his/her problem in this text?

    F. What was your first reaction to this [story / chapter / article]? Please explain using specific examples

    G. What would you say is the main idea of this text?

    H. If you could rename this [story / article / chapter], what would you call it and why?

    A. How did [character/person] change from the beginning of the text to the end of the text?

    B. What is the purpose of this [paragraph / line] on page ____?

    C. What details in the text support the conclusion that _____?

    D. What lesson can we learn from this [article / story / chapter]?

    √E. Choose a line/paragraph from this text that you consider to be very important. Why do you think it is important?

    F. Do you consider this text to be "good literature"? Why or why not?

    G. What is one author's craft technique found in this text that makes the writing lively? Give examples

    H. From whose point of view is this text written? Why do you think the author chose this voice? Give examples from the reading to support your answer

    I. What is the structure of this text? Why do you think the author chose this structure?

    √J. Choose one fact and one opinion in this text. How do you know that one is a fact and the other is an opinion?

    K. How can you tell that the[character / person / author] cared about _____? Use information from the text to support your answer

    A. How is this text similar to another text you read?

    B. What might [character/person] have written in his/her journal after this happened in the text?

    C. List __ questions you would like to ask the author that are not answered in this text. Explain why you would like an answer to each question

    D. Based on information in this text, what would probably have happened if _____?

    E. Using information from the text, how do your visualize this scene?

F. Does [something or someone] in this text remind you of [something or someone] in your own life? Explain or describe

G. If you had been [person/character], how would you have handled the situation when _____?

H. How is [someone or something described in this text] similar to someone or something in our world today?

I. What do you think will happen next? Use information from ths text to support your answer

J. Imagine that you are giving a talk to your class about _____. Using information from the text, write two ideas you would use in this speech

PART ONE

Understanding Written Response to Text

CHAPTER I

A Problem and a Solution

Poorly Written Answers to Comprehension Questions

One of the challenges that middle-grade teachers face on an almost daily basis is how to get kids to write good answers to comprehension questions. Of course, a few students seem able to write eloquently on just about any topic. But too many children repeatedly hand in written responses to comprehension questions that lack organization, elaboration, and fluency.

With the current emphasis on strategic thinking, these inadequately written responses are especially disappointing to teachers. I've visited classrooms in which students as young as third grade sat around and conversed about "text-to-text connections" and "visualizing text passages" like adults participating in a book discussion group. These same children, however, were considerably less competent when the same issues they discussed orally needed a written response.

Three Issues to Ponder

From my own 25 years in an elementary classroom, and from the vantage point of my current role as a university teacher and consultant to school districts, three issues emerge relative to this dilemma:

1. **Should we assume that children can automatically translate their thinking out loud about text into thinking on paper?**

   The short answer is "no." Research in reading gives us a clear picture of the comprehension strategies used by proficient readers that separate them from those students who struggle with understanding (Pearson, 1992). Available to us, as well, are many excellent resources that can guide us as we help our students to become strategic thinkers. (See Part Three: "Books to Teach Comprehension Strategies" for an annotated list of some of my favorite resources on this topic.)

   But is the capacity to talk about text sufficient for producing quality written reflections? We've all seen the evidence that it is not enough:

   - Vague, general answers devoid of specifics.
   - Incomplete answers (even incomplete sentences).
   - Inaccurate answers that miss key text elements.
   - Answers that go around and around, saying the same thing over and over.

2. **Is it important for students to be able to produce well-developed responses to open-ended comprehension questions?**

   Although students at all grade levels have been answering written questions for a long time, the national movement toward more accountability in the schools over the past decade has raised the stakes for such responses. Written answers to comprehension questions on state assessments are frequently used in determining a student's reading level.

   To further complicate the situation, many of those questions relate to expository passages, even at the lower-intermediate level, rather than the more familiar narrative format. *Narrative* is the organizational structure of a *story*, to which many children have been introduced even as very young preschoolers. Youngsters typically have a more difficult time comprehending expository text. This is the format of social studies and science books, encyclopedia articles, and essays. Not only is the expository *structure* something of a mystery (main ideas with supporting details), but kids may not relate to the content — all those new vocabulary words about topics that don't seem to have much personal relevance: far-away countries and planets, or people and events long gone.

   The implications don't stop there. Administrators look not just at individual students, but at each class as a whole. Did your class answer their questions as well as Ms. W's class across the hall, or Mr. T's class across town? Our professional reputation rides on those no-longer-innocent written answers to reading comprehension questions. And our school district's standing rides on how the answers of all our students stack up against those of students in districts across the state.

3. **Is there any way we can teach our students to produce clear, logical, thorough written responses to open-ended comprehension questions once they understand the thinking strategies?**

   I think there is a way. We need to recognize that written response to comprehension questions is a form of expository writing and needs to be explicitly taught. In recent years, we have spent inordinate amounts of instructional time and effort teaching kids the five-paragraph essay, courtesy once again of those high-stakes tests! (In fact, students may readily conclude that the essay is the *only* form of expository writing.) We need to be sure they leave our classrooms with the more accurate view that expository writing has lots of different forms — and written answers to comprehension questions clearly fall within the realm of this genre. Now "all" we need is a method for making this happen.

The Solution: What This Book is About and How to Use it

Teaching Written Response to Text is the resource we need to help all students turn those ho-hum answers into "hooray-for-me" written responses. This book describes a step-by-step method for meeting the needs of students at all learning levels within an intermediate-grade classroom by offering a sequence of instructional support.

Specifically, this book gives you:

- A guide to choosing and using books and choosing and using questions.
- A detailed explanation of explicit instruction and its application to teaching written response to text.
- Instructional supports for teaching written response to text:

   — 30 open-ended questions at three thinking levels. These generic questions may be used with either narrative or expository text.

— Four sequenced instructional supports for each question prepared for immediate classroom use:

    Criteria for quality responses
    Modeled narrative and expository answers
    Answer organizers
    Answer frames

- Several additional resources to enhance the usefulness of this book.

CHAPTER 2

Choosing and Using Books

● ●

As a children's literature junkie, I'm a pretty decent resource when anyone wants a thumbnail sketch of a current book. But I'm often frustrated by the sheer number of great books available, and the scant amount of time in which to share even a tiny percentage of them in the classroom. I've learned to reduce my "book stress" over the years by recognizing that I don't have to actually *teach* every book I love. Experience has taught me that books can be shared in three ways: reading them aloud; talking about them with students; and "teaching" them. I encourage teachers to use each of these ways as a vehicle for improving students' literature response.

Read Books Aloud

I love some books so much that I just have to **read them aloud**. These may be books that are a bit beyond the reading level of my students, but well within their interest level. They may be books where the sound of language contributes in a major way to the text's message. They may be books that elicit laughter or tears, and I want to be there when all those feelings pour out. Or they may not be books at all, but instead a newspaper article, a selection from a nature magazine, a poem, anything that unites us as readers with the common themes of our lives in and out of the classroom. Read-alouds are wonderful sources for literature response because they eliminate whatever challenges children may encounter during the reading process and allow everyone to focus on the thinking process associated with the response itself. Read-alouds give the entire class access to the same piece of literature at the same time. Read-alouds also facilitate whole-group instruction that honors all phases of explicit teaching in a systematic manner.

Talk About Books

We can also share books by **talking about them with our students**. A brief book talk (two minutes?) entices would-be readers by giving them a glimpse of the content along with our enthusiastic endorsement. I tell the whole class about some books and target individual students for others: "Megan, I just finished another story about World War II, and I know you like reading about this topic, too. It's called *Eleanor's Story* (Garner) and it's about an American girl trapped in Germany with her family at the start of the war. Would you like to read my copy?" Megan may want to read *Eleanor's Story* during independent reading time. When she's done, our book conference can include a follow-up written response that, for example, connects this text to another one Megan has read about World War II.

"Teach" Books

Then there are the books to **"teach."** Throughout the year, I investigate several of these with students through serious literature study. These books are selected for their nearly perfect fit with students' reading levels and interests, the concepts they convey, and the craft with which they are written. They are narrative and expository, fiction and nonfiction.

Envision a small group of six to eight students sitting around a table with a teacher, reflecting on the strategies they used to construct meaning about a chapter from the novel, *Number the Stars* (Lowry) or the picture book, *Thank You, Mr. Falker* (Polacco). The teacher participates in the discussion, not to dispense questions, but to model her own thinking as a reader, and to guide students in their use of comprehension strategies.

Some students who are already adept at strategic thinking enjoy the autonomy of literature circles (Daniels, 1994) without the presence of the teacher to guide. With or without the teacher, however, it is in these small-group, directed studies that students monitor their reading strategies most closely. Hence, these books that we "teach" may provide the most natural springboard to written response.

Select Books

It's much easier to suggest *how* books might be linked to written response than it is to identify *which* books to use. (Book selection seems such a personal thing.) Some of my favorites became the models for narrative and expository question responses in this book and are listed with annotations in Part Three: "Books Used for Modeled Responses." Beyond these few texts, it would probably be more productive to identify authors rather than titles.

I'm in love with anything by Cynthia Rylant or Jane Yolen. Even their picture books, short stories, and poems contain enough depth of content and craft techniques to offer middle-grade students multiple opportunities for thoughtful reflection. Poems by Jack Prelutsky seem well-suited to text connections for younger middle-graders, while Sara Holbrook's poetry gives older readers that same kind of connection to teen themes. I choose Shel Silverstein for sure-to-please verse you can visualize.

Other great authors in the narrative category include Patricia Polacco, Faith Ringgold, Chris Van Allsburg, Jon Scieszka, Patricia MacLachlan, Allen Say, Lynne Cherry, Mem Fox, Robert Munsch, Thomas Locker, Kathryn Lasky, Lois Lowry, Phyllis Reynolds Nailor, Walter Dean Myers, Richard Peck, Jerry Spinelli, Barbara Park, Carol Fenner, Christopher Paul Curtis, Mildred D. Taylor, Karen Hesse, Ralph Fletcher, Andrew Clements, Carolyn Coman, Louis Sachar, and my indisputable top choice: Wilson Rawls for his book, *Where the Red Fern Grows.*

Excellent expository and/or nonfiction material is less obvious on the library shelves, but well-written selections do exist. First, however, it's important to make sure we have a clear understanding of the terms *expository* and *nonfiction* so we'll know what we're looking for, and recognize it when we've found it. *Expository* text *explains.* I point out to kids that an easy way to remember this is to look at the beginning of each of the words: *expository* and *explains.* The purpose of the explanation may be to inform or persuade and it may be structured in a variety of ways: cause/effect; problem/solution; description; time order. Textbooks have an expository format as do news articles. Expository text often contains headings and subheadings. Main idea sentences may be stated at the top of a passage, and signal words are present to alert readers to the relationship among ideas (*first, then, in summary,* etc.)

Do note, however, that not all nonfiction is expository. Two exceptions useful to even young children would be *personal narrative* and *biography.* Both of these genres fit the definition of *nonfiction* as they tell about people and events that are *real.* Simultaneously, they also qualify as *narratives,* the stories of people's lives. "Narration is characterized by the passage of time and is organized chronologically." (Freeman, 1998)

When we're in need of expository text for younger students we tend to overlook picture books because we assume picture books are narrative. This is not always so. For example, look at Jane Yolen's *Welcome to the Green House* and *Welcome to the Sea of Sand.* Also, I really like authors Jean Fritz, Gail Gibbons, Seymour Simon, and Russell Freedman. (Lots of picture-support in these texts, too.)

There are some great expository periodicals well matched to middle-grade readers. *Cobblestone* Publications produces a whole family of periodicals. Particularly note-worthy for younger middle-grade readers is *Appleseeds,* targeted to about the fourth-grade reading level, and *Footsteps,* a magazine about African-American history. I also like *Zoobooks,* perfect for life-science themes, and *Kids Discover,* which has issues on almost every theme imaginable.

I prefer the idea of selecting your book *first,* then letting the question grow out of the reading. (Reversing this order seems artificial, and not what "real reading" response is all about.) So what kinds of questions should we ask about these wonderful books?

CHAPTER 3

Choosing and Using Questions

● ●

Ways of Thinking

While it is widely recognized that there are different ways of thinking about text — from literal recall of "the facts" to critical and creative application of abstract concepts, there is decidedly less agreement on *how many* ways of thinking exist and whether or not these "categories" are, or are not, hierarchical in nature. Even if we could somehow all agree on general thinking categories, there would likely still be dissension about what kinds of questions are appropriate for each one.

After agonizing over this for too many hours, and shuffling several questions from one category to another, I devised a framework that makes sense to me — and correlates reasonably well with the comprehension frameworks used by most districts and states. I have decided on three **thinking categories**:

I.   Constructing Basic Meaning
II. Analyzing the Text
III. Text Plus

Constructing Basic Meaning: An Overview

Within this framework, *Constructing Basic Meaning* questions ask students to think about basic narrative story elements: setting, characters, problem, plot, and resolution. These questions also ask about basic expository elements: main idea and supporting details. Students are asked to retell or synthesize information in order to demonstrate their understanding of the text. Generally, these qualify as literal-level questions and do not require students to think too intently about a text's more abstract meaning.

I. Constructing Basic Meaning: The questions

A. According to this text, [who / what / when / where/ how]_____
_____. Why is this important?

B. Choose one word that best describes [name of character/important person], and provide evidence from the text to support your choice.

C. What is the problem or conflict in this text? Give specific details to support your answer.

D. Briefly summarize what happens in this story.

E. How does [character / person] solve his or her problem in this text?

F. What was your first reaction to this [story / article / chapter]? Please explain using specific details.

G. What would you say is the main idea of this [article / chapter / paragraph]?

H. If you could rename this [story / article / chapter], what would you call it and why?

Analyzing the Text: An Overview

I've selected *Analyzing the Text* as a label for the second thinking category. It's a more sophisticated kind of thinking than *Constructing Basic Meaning* because it presumes understanding of basic text features, and it asks students to use this foundation as a springboard to gain insight into the deeper meaning of the author's words. Still, all the clues a student needs to derive an answer lie somewhere within the body of the work. The clues may be hidden "between the lines," and will need to be discovered through inference, but careful contemplation will help readers retrieve pertinent pieces of evidence to create solid written responses.

II. Analyzing the Text: The Questions

  A. How did [character / person] change from the beginning of the text to the end of the text?
  B. What is the purpose of this [paragraph / line] on page _____?
  C. What details in the text support the conclusion that_____?
  D. What lesson can we learn from this [article / story / chapter]?
  E. Choose a [line / paragraph] from this text that you consider to be very important. Why do you think it is important?
  F. Do you consider this text to be "good" literature? Why or why not?
  G. What is one author's craft technique found in this text that makes the writing lively? Give examples.
  H. From whose point of view is this text written? Why do you think the author chose this voice?
  I. What is the structure / organization of this text? Why do you think the author chose this structure?
  J. Choose one fact and one opinion in this text. How do you know that one is a fact and the other is an opinion?
  K. How can you tell that the [character / person / author] cared about _____? Use information from the text to support your answer.

Text Plus: An Overview

Text Plus designates thinking that requires information from the text *plus* background that the reader brings from somewhere else in her life: personal experience, another book, a world event, her imagination, etc. For this kind of thinking, students must integrate what they read with what they already know or what they can imagine. The answer will never be found solely within the text, regardless of how carefully a student reads, nor will it be found solely outside the reading selection. In my opinion, to be a good *reading* comprehension question, the response must rely, at least in part, on the *reading*.

III. Text Plus: The Questions

  A. How is this text similar to another text you read?
  B. What might [character / person] have written in his/her journal after this event happened in the text:_____?

C. List _____ questions you would like to ask the author that are *not* answered in this text. Explain why you would like an answer to each question.

D. Based on information in this text, what probably would have happened if_____?

E. Using information from the text, how do you visualize this scene?

F. Does something in this text remind you of something in your own life? Explain or describe.

G. If you had been [person / character], how would you have handled the situation when_____?

H. How is [someone or something described in this text] similar to someone or something in our world today?

I. What do you think will happen next? Use information from the text to support your answer.

J. Imagine that you are giving a talk to your class about _____. Using information from the text, write two ideas you would use in your speech.

Ask Questions in All Categories

In case you are feeling terribly indignant about the category where certain questions appear, keep in mind that the exact placement is not the key issue here. The important thing is not how we *label* the questions, but that as teachers we provide our students with opportunities to answer *all* of these kinds of questions somewhere within our curriculum. Students at the lower-intermediate level (third and fourth grades) won't be quite as capable of abstract reasoning as readers in the upper-elementary grades and middle school. But *all* children should be given the opportunity to respond to appropriate questions in all three thinking categories.

Typically, teachers spend most of their time on literal (*Constructing Meaning*) questions. This is a good place to begin because children should have a firm foundation in text basics before tackling the deeper thinking required to analyze or apply a text. But don't stop here! Students need as many experiences as we can provide them in interpreting and extending their reading. Be sure to give equal time to *Analyzing the Text* and *Extending the Text* questions. If students can respond *orally* to a given question, they should be able to get that response down on paper, as well.

Seven Comprehension Strategies

Do the questions included here represent every question students will ever encounter as they respond to reading? No, we can think of dozens of derivations to further expand their question-answering repertoire. However, we can feel confident that at the very least we have tapped into the **seven essential comprehension strategies** that empower successful readers (Keene and Zimmermann, 1997). The importance of these strategies remained paramount as I selected appropriate questions to include:

- Determining importance
- Relating the new to the known
- Synthesizing
- Inferring
- Asking questions
- Creating sensory images
- Monitoring for meaning

To learn more about these strategies, see Part Three: "Books to Teach Comprehension Strategies." Meanwhile, raise your level of awareness about how different questions draw upon the use of different strategies. When you select a question, try to identify the strategy involved. A few examples would be:

- Briefly summarize the main idea and supporting details of this [article / chapter / book]. (This question asks students to synthesize what they have read.)
- What is the purpose of this [paragraph / line] on page____? (This question asks students to infer.)
- How is this text similar to another text you read? (This question asks students to relate the new to the known.)

Generic Questions for Narrative and Expository Text

You will note that most of the questions included in this book work for both narrative and expository text. In phrasing the questions, the word *text* is often used in place of *story, chapter, article,* etc. because it can include written material of any genre. Sometimes different options are mentioned within brackets [ ] in a given question to suggest variations specific to one genre or the other.

For example, *"If you had been [person / character] how would you have handled the situation when_____?"* In this case "person" is appropriate for expository text, and "character" is appropriate for a narrative. Additionally, the words in brackets and the blank underlines may be replaced by a particular person or character and a particular event when the teacher uses the question with the selected text: *"If you had been Marian Anderson, how would you have handled the situation when you were denied the right to sing at Constitution Hall?"*

A few of the questions are genre-specific and therefore include a single modeled response. Nearly all of the questions correlate well with both narrative and expository text used in the classroom for reading, social studies, and science instruction. These questions are not intended for use with math content.

Points to Keep in Mind

As you introduce these questions to students, it would be helpful to keep in mind the following points:

These are *open-ended* questions. That is, we are not looking simply for *correct* responses, but rather for *well-developed* responses built upon *details*. Teachers sometimes assume that students understand exactly what the word "details" means. When I see a child's writing piece where the teacher has scrawled across the top "needs more details," I anticipate that there will not be much improvement for this student based on that vague feedback. If this child knew some of the options available to him for adding details, he probably would have put them there in the first place. Please see Part Three: *Details About Details*. These strategies will be useful for students responding to open-ended comprehension questions — and other kinds of expository writing, as well.

Celebrate quality, not quantity. You should *talk* about many book-related issues. But when it's time to respond in writing, narrow the focus to *one* special question. What *one* question do you really want your students to reflect on after reading and discussing a particular book or part of a book?

For example, at the conclusion of *Charlotte's Web* (E. B. White): What details in the text support the conclusion that Charlotte was a really great friend to Wilbur? If students can answer that, they have found their way to one of the central themes of that story. Or, for *The Velveteen Rabbit*

(Margery Williams): How did the Boy change from the beginning of the text to the end? Isn't that the most significant question we could ask readers about that text?

Give students the opportunity to respond orally to a question before expecting them to respond in writing. Many children, especially struggling readers or ESOL students, see failure glaring back at them when they produce written work that they or the teacher view as inadequate. Experimenting with thoughts out loud establishes a little more confidence before putting pen to paper.

Be sure that the question you've selected is a good match for the book you've chosen. One way to be certain about this is to write the response yourself using either the Answer Organizer or the Answer Frame (explained in Chapter 5) for the question you've selected. Adhere to the criteria and model, just as you would expect your students to do. If you breeze through this task, chances are good that your students will be successful as well. If you have trouble, it would be wise to shop around for a question with better "connectability." For example, asking, "From whose point of view is this text written?" about a chapter from a social studies text with a third-person narrator isn't going to be very effective with most young readers because they will not recognize a distinctive voice in such material. This would be a terrific question, however, for a picture book like *The Tree That Would Not Die*, by Ellen Levine which is, in fact, told from the tree's perspective.

Introduce one question at a time and practice it until students are proficient in responding to it. As with all explicit instruction, the lesson must be taught, practiced, and (ideally) over-learned to the point of *independent* application. (Much more about that in the next chapter.)

CHAPTER 4

Understanding Explicit Instruction

●●●

Getting Started with Explicit Instruction

In my youthful, more innocent days as a teacher I honestly thought that when I gave kids good books to read and good questions to answer about those books, that I was *teaching* comprehension. I've since figured out that in so doing, I was actually *testing* comprehension. "Good" teaching, which I define as *explicit* teaching, is about much more than just assigning and assessing.

Explicit instruction is more complex than we might wish it to be, which is why good written responses (and other quality student products) often elude us. I was introduced to explicit instruction a couple of decades ago through the work of Madeline Hunter. She referred to this as "teaching for mastery" — a different label for essentially the same concept. Since then, I've encountered the explicit teaching model in a variety of forms, and have examined it through the eyes of several scholar-practitioners.

I've included an annotated list of a few of my favorite references related to explicit teaching in Part Three, "Resources for Explicit Teaching." The perspective in each text is unique, but one idea is central to *all* of these sources: Effective instruction requires more than a solid command of the *content*. It is a function of the *process* of teaching, as well. That is, the same basic principles may be applied to teaching a lesson within *any* academic discipline. The process of explicit teaching in *writing* looks a lot like the process of explicit teaching in *science* or *math*.

Envision these scenarios: You step into a fifth-grade classroom in which children are engaged in an animated discussion of the Holocaust after watching a video clip of interviews with Holocaust survivors; tomorrow they will begin reading their next novel, *Number the Stars* (Lowry). Now, imagine visiting a fourth-grade classroom and watching a teacher give a top-rate explanation of how to determine the topic sentence in a paragraph. You enter another classroom and a teacher is demonstrating fluent oral reading of a poem. In a sixth-grade classroom, you see a teacher distributing a story map for students to complete after reading a literature selection in their basal anthology.

You have just watched teachers:

- Motivate students and build their background knowledge
- Explain a new skill
- Model a quality product
- Provide guided practice

Did you witness effective instruction in each of these classrooms? Used separately, these instructional practices will not get the job done. Used *together*, though, they make a powerful instructional package.

Explicit instruction (also known as "direct instruction") is a sequence of supports: first *setting a purpose for learning*, then *telling* students what to do, then *showing* them how to do it, and finally *guiding* their hands-on application of the new learning. Explicit instruction begins with **setting the stage for learning**, followed by a clear **explanation** of what to do (telling), followed by **modeling** of the process (showing), followed by multiple opportunities for **practice** (guiding) until independence is attained. Explicit instruction moves systematically from extensive teacher input and little student responsibility initially — to total student responsibility and minimal teacher involvement at the conclusion of the learning cycle.

Setting the Stage for Learning

Instruction should actually begin long before *the lesson*. Diving headlong into the content spells disaster for many students, especially those who struggle with learning. Do they know enough about the topic to build upon that foundation? Do they know *why* they're reading a particular text? Do they even *care* about this content?

The most logical place for any lesson to begin is by explaining the *purpose* of the activity:

- "Today we are going to work on_____."
- "By the time we have finished, you will be better at _____."

Effective teachers then get their kids to *care* about the forthcoming lesson by connecting it to their interests, their background knowledge, the previous day's lesson, or all of the above: "Remember yesterday when we talked about whether *Where the Red Fern Grows* was "good" literature? Remember what a terrific job you did finding proof in the story for your opinions? Well, today I'm going to show you how to organize your response *in writing* so it contains that same great elaboration."

Explaining: Telling Students *What* to Do

Once you've identified *what* you're going to accomplish, and *why* it's important to pursue this goal, your next mission is to answer *how*: How will you get the job done? Effective teachers present no-frills explanations that give students *just enough* information to cover the basics and get them started on the task. This is one of those times when *less* is *more*. Resist the urge to ramble on about all the fine points of the new skill; there will be plenty of time for that later when the foundation has been built. Also, save for another time those cute little anecdotes about *your* experience learning this skill in the third grade (which will divert their attention from the lesson at hand.)

Most of all, though, refrain from beginning with a warning about how *hard* the new skill will be for students to learn. I have been in so many classrooms where teachers, in an effort to get everyone to listen up, precede their explanation with, "Now, this thing we're going to learn today is very hard, so if you don't pay attention, you're not going to get it." The only word kids hear in that sentence is *hard*, which causes many of them to tune out right then. They think, "I'll never understand this anyway, so why bother to make the effort."

A good teacher knows that her job is to provide an explanation that is simple and direct enough to make the learning accessible to *all* of the students in the class. She also knows the power of a positive approach.

- "You won't believe how easy this is going to be..."
- "I can show you an easy way to..."
- "You may be shocked at how quickly you catch on to this..."
- "I'm going to go slowly and help you every step of the way. I promise that I won't let you get lost."

Now, students feel empowered to face the challenge of new learning. They feel safe that you are there for them if the going gets rough.

So what does a *good* explanation involve?

- Divide the task into a few component steps. (Three to five steps is a good number; more than that may signal that the new learning is complex enough to warrant more than one lesson.)
- Tell the students how many steps will be involved. ("I'm going to tell you how to do this job in three simple steps.")
- Present the steps both orally and visually to meet the needs of children with different modality strengths, and to provide extra reinforcement. I like to write the steps one at a time on a transparency as I talk about them. (Later I transfer what I've written onto a large chart for display in the classroom, or onto sheets of paper so everyone can have their own copies.)
- State the steps as clearly as possible. Do this by using short sentences devoid of complicated jargon and multiple clauses. Begin each sentence with a verb. Number the steps so that students will understand the sequence and recognize the transitions: "1. Write a topic sentence that includes the name of the character and his or her important trait."

If the steps to achieve the goal are not identified, students' replication of the process will occur more by hit-or-miss than by actual design, even when subsequent lesson components are solid. The most perceptive students in the class will hit the target intuitively; the rest will most likely miss it, for they never understood in the first place what they were supposed to do.

Modeling: Showing Students How to Reach Their Goal

Based on my observations, many teachers appear to believe that *explaining* is synonymous with *instruction*. But good instruction does not end with a good explanation. When the extent of the instruction is *only* an explanation, without modeling or guided practice, teachers have no idea whether or not students understand the lesson content until it's too late. Just hearing or reading the directions is not enough for most middle-grade learners. Despite your best efforts, cries of "I don't get it" may echo throughout the classroom from frustrated kids (and teachers) who already feel like failures before they've even begun the assignment. This kind of panic can be eliminated with attention to the next step in explicit instruction: modeling.

Modeling offers children the opportunity to watch the process unfold before their eyes. Modeling means that the teacher engages in whatever is involved in the learning task *exactly* as students will be expected to perform it. It is so important that the model adheres to the steps delineated in the explanation and maps directly onto the learning task.

While this may seem obvious, it is not always what happens in a classroom. I have watched teachers provide great step-by-step explanations, and then ignore these criteria with their own model. I have watched teachers do fabulous demonstrations of a lesson in, for example, editing for correct punctuation. Then they hand students a follow-up activity sheet that may draw upon the same concept, but approaches the task from an entirely different perspective. Modeling is the visual (and sometimes oral) link between the explanation that precedes it, and the students' guided application of the process, which will follow.

I find that I am able to use the modeling portion of the lesson most meaningfully when students are gathered around me and not dispersed throughout the classroom at their desks. We feel like a group then. Although I need to do a large percentage of the talking, I want to be able to connect with the kids, to see their eyes (alert and focused, or adrift and glazed-over). I want their informal input as often as possible, which may be as subtle as a flickering smile to show me they're "getting it," or a hand raised tentatively to ask a question. It may *seem* that the teacher is doing most of the work during modeling, but this is *not* a spectator sport. Good teachers find lots of little ways to bring children into the process to keep them actively involved. A few of these ways include:

- Asking students to underline a portion of text on the chalkboard or overhead transparency — the topic sentence, a supporting quote, a detail that tells where or when, etc.
- Asking students to tell you what kind of punctuation to use at the end of a sentence: "Am I asking or telling here? What kind of punctuation should we use?"

- Asking students to suggest a synonym for a word you've included in the response: " 'Winnie-the-Pooh was fat.' Can anyone think of a more interesting describing word?"
- Asking students to check the text for you because you need to prove...
- Asking students to read the completed response aloud with you to make sure it sounds good and makes sense. Then ask for possible revisions.

Without such active involvement, modeling will not achieve its intended purpose.

Guiding a Little or a Lot

I like graphic organizers and frames because they work! It's easy for teachers to find or create templates to match nearly any format that students need. These templates simplify the task of representing knowledge on paper by providing graphic cues. Graphic organizers and frames are helpful *instructional aids* that assist children in moving quite securely from teacher-control of the lesson, toward their own independent application of the new learning.

Graphic organizers are not, however, a *substitute* for instruction — which is sometimes the way they are used! When students receive a graphic organizer or frame to complete for a text selection without sufficient explanation or modeling *beforehand*, they have no idea *why* they are using that particular format for their literature response.

To complicate matters, students are often successful with the graphic because it is so carefully guided. Teachers, of course, are elated to see such promising performance and expect this expertise to translate into high test scores on comparable material. Unfortunately, this is an unreasonable expectation.

If students are to do well on a task in a testing situation, (in this case, respond to open-ended comprehension questions) they need to have *heard* the explanation, *seen* the model, *practiced* with the organizer or frame as many times as needed — and then worked backward, removing one support at a time. After enough trials with the graphic aid, the teacher should take that away and expect children to be able to answer the question with just a review of the model and the answer criteria. Eventually, the model should disappear, as well, and at some point, even the answer criteria should not be needed. When students are capable of responding to the question all by itself without the benefit of instructional supports, that's when they're truly independent.

That's when they're ready for the test, for on the test all they will get to guide them is "the question."

Putting It All Together

With explicit instruction, teachers have a great deal of responsibility to monitor students' needs and provide the kind of scaffolding most appropriate at any point throughout the learning process. But students have a responsibility, too. They must realize that at some point they will be expected to perform the task *by themselves* and they should, thus, work systematically toward achieving that goal.

At the outset of any lesson — before I explain, before I model, before I distribute the organizer or frame — I make this shared responsibility clear to the students: "I'm going to teach you how to write a good answer to this question. First I'll *tell* you what to do. Then I'll *show* you how to do it. Then what do you think I'll expect you to do?" They quickly discern that they will need to produce something themselves. "So while I'm teaching you, what should you be doing?" The consensus is "pay attention." "Yes," I affirm directing their attention toward *purposeful* learning: You should be thinking about how *you* will write *your* answer when it's *your* turn."

The following graphic illustrates this model of explicit instruction which is used here to teach written response to text. The instructional supports in Part Two of this book adhere to this instructional model (see Figure 4.1).

Figure 4.1

The Explicit Teaching of Written Response to Text

Explicit Teaching   **Student Independence**

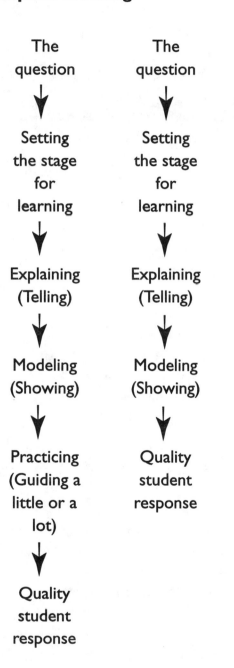
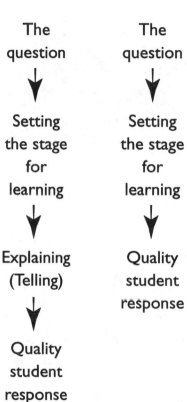
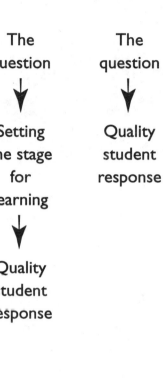

The question	The question	The question	The question	The question
↓	↓	↓	↓	↓
Setting the stage for learning	Setting the stage for learning	Setting the stage for learning	Setting the stage for learning	Quality student response
↓	↓	↓	↓	
Explaining (Telling)	Explaining (Telling)	Explaining (Telling)	Quality student response	
↓	↓	↓		
Modeling (Showing)	Modeling (Showing)	Quality student response		
↓	↓			
Practicing (Guiding a little or a lot)	Quality student response			
↓				
Quality student response				

CHAPTER 5

Applying Explicit Instruction to Written Response to Text: Telling, Showing, Guiding

•••

Explaining the Criteria for Good Answers: Telling Students *What* to Do

As discussed in the previous chapter, the first component of an explicit lesson after the teacher has motivated students and tapped their background knowledge, is to specify the criteria required to attain the designated learning goal. (Here's how you get "the *A*.") In the case of written response to text, that goal is to write a high-quality response to an open-ended reading comprehension question.

You will note as you examine the answer criteria for questions in this book that a "quality response" typically involves a topic sentence, some details from the text, a supporting quote, and sometimes a concluding statement. The specifications for individual questions are variations on this general theme and are intended only as approximate guidelines. (For a more comprehensive look at writing standards for different grade levels see Part Three: "Grade Level Expectations for Written Response to Text.") Of course, writing improves as writers mature. Standards for third graders will be a lot less rigorous than expectations for students in the eighth grade.

I always tell students: when in doubt, "three" is a good number — three reasons, three details, three important points. However, it's *your* class; *you* need to decide whether these criteria are just right for your kids, or if they need a bit of modifying. For instance, students in the older grades might be asked to supply more supporting evidence, while finding a single relevant detail may be appropriate for younger children. Whatever you decide to include as "non-negotiable," go over the plan step-by-step with the class: "Here's what I want you to include in this answer and the way I'd like you to write it:

First, you...

Next, you...

Then, you...

Finally, you..."

Writing the steps on the chalkboard as you describe them, or making a transparency out of the pertinent page in this book are ways to share the needed information with students. Ideally, you'll also provide the information on a large easy-to-read classroom chart for reference later, or the same page from this book duplicated and distributed to all students to keep in their writing folders. Avoid handing the duplicated page to students and telling them to read it and figure it out for themselves.

If you want your children to hand in written responses that approach your expectations, think through an assignment before introducing it to them and be able to identify *exactly* what needs to be done to complete the activity successfully. This *telling* step (although the telling is also in written form) meets the needs of the auditory learners in our classrooms who need to *hear* what to do in order to succeed. It allows *all* kids to feel safe in the knowledge that "this is what you need to do to get a good grade on this assignment." Without such clarity, our students are often (quite legitimately) confused. What does Teacher want?

Even worse, without conscious consideration of the criteria, Teacher is often confused, too. Sometimes we approach a set of students' papers the way we approach a trip to the mall to locate the perfect present for Aunt Charlotte's birthday: we're not quite sure what we're looking for, but hope that somehow we'll know when we've found it. In both cases, a more systematic plan gets the job done more efficiently and effectively.

One final word-to-the-wise about the criteria: There may be a couple of excellent writers in your class who feel too confined by such a finely delineated set of writing standards. You most likely know who these kids are already because they write great responses to literature quite independently — without your guidance. Honor that competence and independence by allowing them the freedom to continue to set their own standards. As with all good instruction, *Teaching Written Response to Text* is for students who need teacher support to learn a skill, not for students who have already achieved that goal.

Modeling a Good Answer: Showing Students How to Reach Their Goal

The first question teachers usually ask me when I present this strategy sequence is, "If you show the kids a good answer, won't they just copy yours?" Yes, they probably will. That's why I model the answer with one text, and ask them to answer the same question for a different selection.

For instance, the question might ask, "Briefly summarize what happens in this story." I could model this response with the answer in this book for the fable, *The Bad Kangaroo*. The same set of response criteria would work for *any* story. So, students could watch me construct my answer for *The Bad Kangaroo* and then answer this same question ("Briefly summarize what happens in this story") for any text that they had read, using my model as a guide. Teaching in this way allows us to not only teach *about* the literature, but also to teach *through* the literature: Can students transfer what they learn through the study of one book to another context? Returning to our same example, I'm more concerned about whether kids can summarize *any* story, not just *The Bad Kangaroo*. To move toward this goal, I want them to be able to form a clear *visual image* of a quality response, with all of its components. This visual representation, or **model**, of what to do seems to be the missing link in many teaching situations.

There are a variety of ways we can incorporate this modeling link. I think the most effective modeling strategy is to actually construct the model with your students. You already have the model from the book. Think aloud as you record it one sentence at a time.

"Let's see, I need to start with a topic sentence that tells the name of the person and his/her important trait. Okay, if I was writing about Thomas Edison, I first need to decide on a trait that really describes him.....Hmmmm, in this article it shows how he was very, very curious, so I could say, "I think the word 'curious' really describes Thomas Edison." Did I meet the criteria here for a topic sentence?" Give students the opportunity to reflect and reply.

This accomplishes several things. Students have witnessed not only the construction of a good topic sentence, but they've also gotten an insider's view of the strategies you used to develop that sentence. We want to make our thinking visible to students because we want them to employ similar strategies as they fashion their own answers. Furthermore, constructing the model with students places them in more of a participatory role. You can ask for their input. You can ask them to monitor whether you've met the criteria. You can ask for possible revisions to make the response more fluent. Even a little involvement goes a long way in getting students engaged in the learning process. If the modeling is done entirely by the *teacher,* students can slip too easily into a passive role.

Another, even simpler means of modeling is to duplicate from this book the narrative or expository modeled response that correlates with the question under study. Read it sentence by sentence with your students showing how each part of the response maps onto the "how to" steps set out in the criteria. Engaging in this process yourself with the response on a transparency will allow you to highlight different sections of the answer in different colors — which will provide still more visual cues.

In my experience, using models of narrative and expository selections that students have not yet read works fine. The focus is on the *process* rather than the content, so there is no real need for prior knowledge of the text. However, most models have been created with materials at a fourth- or fifth-grade reading level and interest levels between third- and seventh-grade. If you think that is too high or too low for your students, there is another modeling option you might want to consider.

You can use the response criteria for your focus question, and design your own model based on a narrative or expository piece your class has already read — one that is matched to their developmental needs as readers and writers. Always try to create your models to approximate the writing skill level of students in your grade.

As I crafted the answers for questions in this book, I tried to think like a 10- or 11-year-old and write what might come from his/her pen. I figured children should see what a well-developed response should look like, but I tried not to write in a way that would intimidate middle-grade students. After seeing the model, children should think, "I can do that," not, "I could *never* write like you do." In an effort to sound "real," if not eloquent, I used language and concepts that could have come from the minds and mouths of readers in an upper-elementary classroom — before polishing or publishing. (Realistically, written answers to comprehension questions do not face the same scrutiny with regard to "beautiful writing" that we expect of other genres.) I did make sure that the words covered all the key elements of an accurate, organized, thorough, and fluent response. If these answers don't sound like *your* students' written reflections about text at the present time, maybe they could be viewed as a worthy goal to try to attain. (See Part Three: Grade Level Expectations for Written Response to Text to get a better sense of where your students are along the writing continuum).

Guiding Good Answers with a Little Graphic Support: The Answer Organizer

We want students to construct responses that are accurate, organized, thorough, and fluent. *Accuracy* is a function of comprehension — and comprehension needs to be addressed before writing about text can begin. We really cannot expect students to respond to literature they don't understand. (See Part Three: "Books to Teach Comprehension Strategies.")

Thoroughness, organization, and *fluency*, however, is more *writing* issues than *reading* issues, and can get a big boost from graphic support. (See Chapter Six for more about each of these writing traits.) Most students, when first introduced to a particular question and modeled response, will need some form of graphic aid to help them get their answer onto paper in logical order.

The least structured level of graphic support is the **Answer Organizer**. When you look at the criteria and compare it to the Answer Organizer, you'll notice a striking resemblance. This is not just a coincidence. The Answer Organizer simply takes the criteria and breaks it into bite-sized chunks so that those students who tend to get confused, overwhelmed, or otherwise off-track can remain focused.

Point this out to students. "Look, it's asking you here to write a topic sentence that states the main idea. Make sure you *only* write your topic sentence in this space. On this second set of lines, write a sentence that explains how you know this is the main idea. You're going to have to think about this. Will the reason be stated right in the text, or will you have to figure something out that is not stated directly? In this final section, find and write two or three details that *show* this is the main idea. Remember, your details need to *prove* your point about the main idea. Also remember that one way of showing proof is by using a quote directly from the text."

Carving the answer into its component parts helps students respond to one piece completely before moving on to the next. It also helps the teacher identify portions of an answer that are complete and those that are vague or lack sufficient detail. As an optional final step, students can transcribe their answers from the Answer Organizer to a blank sheet of paper so their finished work will look more like a traditional "connected narrative" response.

Guiding Good Answers with a Lot of Graphic Support: The Answer Frame

An even more substantial level of concrete guidance is offered by the **Answer Frame**. In this format, **sentence stems** are provided and children essentially "fill in the blanks." The students receive direction not only in the sequencing of tasks, but also in translating thoughts into words. This is helpful to students who would not succeed any other way. With this much support, they, too, can write respectable responses to reading comprehension questions. However, we need to remember that while this may be a good place to begin, it is not a good place to end.

I am reminded of a quote by E. M. Forster: "Spoon feeding in the long run teaches us nothing but the shape of the spoon." In the long run, we need to gradually wean students from this level of dependency. We need to build on their successful Answer Frame responses until we can remove that level of scaffolding and help them become comfortable with an Answer Organizer. Then we should work backward even more until they can write responses with just a model for guidance. And if we really persist, someday they'll understand the criteria well enough to read a question by themselves and write an answer that is complete, correct, and logical. And all the teacher will need to do at that point is watch!

Trouble-shooting Problem Areas

Nearly all students will be able to function with an Answer Frame. But if even this proves too challenging, what do you do then? One possibility is to complete the frame together with a small group of students, repeating the process until everyone understands what to do and can accomplish at least that task independently.

And what if they *still* just don't know what to write on those lines? If students struggle even with the assistance of these graphic aids, it's probably because their real deficiency is in the area of *reading comprehension* strategies rather than *writing* strategies. While this book is not intended to *teach* reading comprehension, it can help you identify the source of the comprehension problem.

Do some students have a hard time coming up with a topic sentence?
A topic sentence is generally derived from understanding the main idea of a text (or section of text). Main ideas are usually *inferred* rather than stated. So, trouble with topic sentences is probably a symptom of poor inferential reasoning. These students may benefit from more instruction and practice with the use of the *inferring* strategy as a way to construct meaning.

Do some students have a hard time choosing details that support their topic sentence? Students who have difficulty with this likely are the same ones who underline every line of print on a page with a yellow highlighter. They can't distinguish the important details from "everything else." Figuring out which details are truly central to a point — and which ones are "fluff" — is critical to good comprehension. These students need more work with the strategy of *determining importance.*

Do some students have difficulty finding an exact quote that proves a point? Documenting a claim with specific textual support used to be introduced at about the high school level. Now we ask third graders to do this same thing — and they're probably not going to figure it out on their own. We need to make sure our instruction helps them meet this challenge.

To that end, a separate "Prove It!" worksheet designed to address this need is presented in Part Three. This sheet provides students with practice in finding detail sentences in a text that support a general statement. The teacher fills in the page number and "Prove It!" point. Example: "Find evidence on page 14 that Grip was a very friendly dog." The student's job is to find a piece of text that provides evidence of that point: *"He frisked, he wriggled, he wagged his tail."* The "Prove It!" worksheet can be used as a constructing-meaning activity to accompany your reading or content area curricula — with or without open-ended comprehension questions. Use this opportunity, too, to reinforce appropriate punctuation, especially those ornery quotation marks.

Do some students have difficulty constructing a concluding statement that pulls their response together? These students would benefit from some help in the area of *synthesizing.* Ultimately, kids need one of those "light bulb" experiences, one of those "now-I-see-what-all-of-this-means" moments that can take shape in a wrap-up sentence of about 12 words.

Do some students know what to write on the lines — but demonstrate extreme deficiencies in writing conventions: grammar, usage, spelling? This area, too, is beyond the purview of this book. However, it would be helpful to turn to Part Three: "Grade Level Expectations for Written Response to Text" to evaluate the match between the student(s) in question and the approximate level of writing development. If a third grader only remembers to capitalize proper names and the first word in every sentence, we're not too worried for she's developmentally on-target for her age and grade level. If we observe this same behavior in an eighth grader, there's more cause for concern.

Keep in mind that you'll save yourself a great deal of stress if you address writing (and all learning) challenges incrementally. Look less at the *ultimate* goal, and more at what you need to do *next* to move a student forward. With consistent effort, the end goal will eventually take care of itself.

The Instructional Sequence: A Synthesis

The goal of this book is to prepare you to teach written response to text. If you've succeeded in synthesizing the information on the preceding pages, you're most likely close to that goal right now. After reflecting upon the suggestions offered here, you may already have a plan for how you can use this text meaningfully with the students *you* teach.

It was not my intent to dictate a prescribed method of implementing these instructional strategies. I think effective teaching occurs most readily when a teacher interprets best practice based on the unique needs of her own classroom.

Still, for those educators who are new to their role, or just feel the need for a bit more direction, I offer the following instructional sequence:

1. **Read a text** aloud to students, or have them read the text themselves either independently, or using a small-group guided format.
2. **Discuss the text** with students to be sure that they can construct basic meaning, and can use their reading strategies both to analyze and apply the text.
3. **Identify the one *significant* question** you want students to respond to in writing, and be sure this is addressed in your discussion of the text.
4. **Prepare your lesson materials** from *Teaching Written Response to Text* to teach written response to your identified question.
5. **Plan your lesson** (which will need approximately one class period at the middle school level, and perhaps a little more time at earlier grade levels.) The lesson should incorporate all components of explicit instruction.

6. **Introduce the lesson** by identifying the goal (responding to the identified question), helping students to care about the new learning, and accessing and building their background knowledge. (About 5-7 minutes)
7. **Explain the criteria** for a quality response to your question. (About 5-7 minutes)
8. **Model a quality response** to the question, making both the process and the product visible to students. (About 10-12 minutes)
9. **Provide for guided practice** using either the Answer Organizer or Answer Frame. Some students my be comfortable with the organizer, and others may require the more specific guidance of the Frame. Most students would benefit from one of these forms of graphic support, at least initially. Use your judgment. (About 15-20 minutes)
10. **Provide for closure** by having some of the students read their responses aloud. It is also helpful to them as a class to reflect on the process by which they constructed their responses so they can be aware of their thinking, and replicate the process the next time. (5-7 minutes)
11. **Assess students' written responses** in order to diagnose learning needs and inform subsequent instruction. Students' level of proficiency in responding to the question should guide your *next* lesson in written response to text: Are students ready to address a different question? Do they need continued practice with the same question? What *individual* needs present themselves as you evaluate their work?

As you incorporate the teaching of written response to text into the life of your classroom in a systematic manner, you will make adjustments to this set of procedures until the instruction feels just right for you and your students.

In my experience, most students need about four or five opportunities to respond to a question using the organizer before attempting the answer on a blank sheet of paper. At that point I just review the model and criteria before children pick up their pens to write. This represents a giant step toward independence. By seeing how long it takes your students to reach independence on a single question, you can estimate the number of questions you can reasonably address between September and June. Chapter Six provides help to establish written response expectations for both teachers and students.

CHAPTER 6

Establishing Written Response Expectations for Teachers and Students

• •

How do we evaluate whether students are truly "making the grade" in written response, and whether teachers are, in fact, doing all they can to make the teaching of written response a regular part of their literacy curriculum? To answer the first part of that question, we can look at grade level expectations for writing competencies, and from that, generate a rubric that helps measure written response performance with a numberical score. To help you develop a comprehensive school or district plan for instruction in written response, the scope and sequence that follows offers a continuum for instituting written response curriculum over a range of grades, from the primary level through middle school.

Grade Level Expectations for Written Response to Text

Students' acquisition of writing skills occurs along a continuum. That is, they must master *basic* writing competencies before moving on to the kind of craft we expect when we open a novel or read a newspaper. Skills of written expression begin to develop when a young child picks up a crayon or other writing implement and scribbles his first marks onto a piece of paper (or his bedroom wall). A comprehensive continuum of written language skills could begin with that initial scribble — but that would serve no purpose in this book.

Below is a continuum of competencies that specifically targets the writing development of intermediate grade students as they learn to respond to open-ended comprehension questions. Most students in the third and fourth grades will perform at a **beginning** level of text response. While this is acceptable for this developmental stage, the questions we should always ask ourselves are: What's *next* for this student? What can I do as a teacher to help this student reach a standard at the next level?

The instructional supports in this book (the criteria, the modeled responses, the Answer Organizers, and Answer Frames) are generally targeted to the **Developing** level, or the kind of written responses to text we expect students to be able to produce in the fifth and sixth grades. Writing at this stage tends to be efficient, though not necessarily eloquent.

Advanced text response, which may characterize the writing of seventh and eighth graders, is quite complex with excellent organization, thorough elaboration, and lots of author's craft techniques for added fluency. Writing at this level sounds so good that we have an urge to share it with someone else!

The following writing characteristics for each developmental stage may *loosely* be regarded as expectations for different grade levels. They are adapted from criteria established in *The Author's Profile* (Beaver).

Grades Three and Four: Beginning

- The **main idea** is clearly established in a topic sentence.
- One or two **details** are provided.
- **Evidence** is provided that is relevant.
- The **conclusion** makes reference to the main idea.
- In general, **sentences** are correctly structured.
- Ideas in a **paragraph** are all related to the same subject.
- The **language used** is appropriate for the piece.
- In general, the following **punctuation** is used correctly: ending marks.
- In general, the following are **capitalized** correctly: sentences, names.
- There is enough **conventional spelling** for easy reading.

Grades Five and Six: Developing

- The **main idea** is clearly established in a topic sentence, and is stated in a way to get the reader's attention.
- Two or three **details** are provided that are directly connected to the main idea.
- **Evidence** is provided that is relevant and documented with a direct quote from the text.
- The **conclusion** makes reference to the main idea and establishes closure.
- In general, **sentences** are correctly structured and begin in a variety of ways.
- **Paragraphs** are logically organized around a single subject, and they are indented.
- The **language** used is appropriate, specific, and clear.
- In general, the following **punctuation** is used correctly: ending marks, apostrophes, commas.
- In general, the following are **capitalized** correctly: sentences, names, titles.
- The piece is generally **spelled** conventionally.

Grades Seven and Eight: Advanced

- The **main idea** is clearly established in a topic sentence, is stated in a way to get the reader's attention, and may be written as a thesis in an introductory paragraph.
- Three **details** are provided that are directly connected to the main idea and contain elaboration.
- **Evidence** is provided that is relevant, documented with a direct quote from the text, and represents varied craft techniques. (See "Details about Details.")
- The **conclusion** makes reference to the main idea, establishes closure creatively, and may be presented as a separate paragraph that also reviews the main points.
- In general, **sentences** are correctly structured, begin in a variety of ways, and vary in length.
- The piece usually contains several **paragraphs** which are logically ordered and indented, each with a topic sentence and supporting details.
- The **language** is appropriate, specific, clear, and is distinctly personal.

- In general, the following **punctuation** is used correctly: ending marks, apostrophes, commas, quotation marks, colons, hyphens, and parentheses.
- In general, the following are **capitalized** correctly: sentences, names, titles, quotations, special effects.
- The piece is consistently **spelled** conventionally, including some specialized vocabulary.

For those times when it would be useful to have a score for children's written responses, teachers can examine writing at a student's developmental level (beginning, developing, or advanced) and decide how an answer measures up against four traits: accuracy, organization, thoroughness, and fluency. A four-point scale is described here, although the range could be adjusted up or down depending on a teacher's preferences or a district's requirements.

Written Response Rubric

4 = Superior

Superior responses demonstrate a high level of comprehension of the text, including the capacity to construct basic meaning, interpret and think critically, as well as the ability to represent that understanding in writing. All four of the response traits are strong and consistent.

Accuracy: The answer is <u>accurate</u> according to developmental level expectations.

The answer is clearly based on events in the text that really happened, correctly represents factual information, and formulates reasonable inferences.

Organization: The answer is logically <u>organized</u> according to developmental level expectations.

The answer follows the steps specified in the response criteria or uses another sequential structure that makes sense to the reader.

Thoroughness: The answer is <u>thorough</u> according to developmental level expectations.

The answer meets all criteria for details and elaboration specified for the response to a particular question, and the details show a close, careful reading of the text.

Fluency: The answer is <u>fluent</u> according to developmental level expectations.

> The answer demonstrates appropriate competence with grammar, usage, writing conventions, vocabulary, and language structure.

2 = Basic

Basic responses demonstrate some comprehension, but show gaps in understanding of the text and/or lack of proficiency in responding to the text in writing.

Accuracy: The answer is <u>partially accurate</u> according to developmental level expectations.

> The answer shows some confusion about events or information described in the text, and inferences may be "far-fetched" or not tied directly to the content of the reading.

Organization: The answer is <u>marginally organized</u> according to developmental level expectations.

> The answer may begin in a logical fashion, but loses its focus, or the parts may all be present, but are not well-sequenced.

Thoroughness: The answer is <u>more general than specific</u> according to developmental level expectations, and hence, lacks thoroughness.

> The answer contains some details and elaboration, but the student has missed or has neglected to include enough evidence from the text to sufficiently support a general statement or main idea.

Fluency: The answer is <u>somewhat fluent</u> according to developmental level expectations.

> The answer is generally able to be read and understood, but may show more carelessness or lack of proficiency in the use of grammar, usage, writing conventions, vocabulary, and language structure than is appropriate for a student at this level.

0 = Deficient

Deficient responses demonstrate confusion or lack of understanding about the meaning of the text, and/or, significant lack of skill in crafting a written response.

Accuracy: The answer is clearly <u>inaccurate</u> and is well below the range of developmental level expectations.

> The answer does not indicate that the student has constructed basic meaning from the text, either explicitly stated information or inferred relationships among ideas. The answer may point to problems that go deeper than comprehension, perhaps insufficient word identification skills.

Organization: The answer has <u>no organizational framework</u> and is well below the range of developmental level expectations.

> The answer may be too sparse to provide a sense of organization, or it may be very long, and repetitive, saying the same thing over and over in a variety of ways, or it may be largely incoherent with no sense of direction.

Thoroughness: The answer is <u>vague and/or irrelevant</u> and is well below the range of developmental level expectations.

> The answer may be so general, far-fetched, or so loosely tied to the text that it is hard to tell whether the student has even done the reading.

Fluency: The answer is <u>nearly incomprehensible</u> because of written language deficits and is well below the range of developmental level expectations.

> The answer shows extreme lack of skill in communicating ideas in writing, and may be a signal that serious intervention beyond the scope of written response instructional supports is in order.

Of course many responses fall into the "gray range": not quite *superior*, but more than *basic*, or not totally *deficient*, but less acceptable than a score of "2" would imply. For those responses, there's a "1" or "3". A general impression of the way all four traits work together in a given response provides the student with a <u>holistic</u> score. A more sophisticated evaluation could examine each trait individually, with an analytic <u>scoring</u> option. For example, a student might receive a "4" in *accuracy*, a "3" in *organization*, a "3" in *thoroughness*, and a "2" in *fluency*. It is important to remember that regardless of whether your evaluation is holistic or analytical, the issue at hand is not really the score a student receives, but the information that score supplies for identifying the student's strengths and needs and suggesting an appropriate next step in instruction.

Implementing a Written Response Curriculum for Your School or District

It is impossible to teach all of these text responses to your class in one academic year. A more realistic and effective approach is to decide which responses you will teach at each grade level within your school or school district so that at some point students will have attained independence on all of the questions.

If teachers at different grade levels coordinate their efforts, students' knowledge of response strategies will become cumulative. For example, if third-grade teachers introduce the "summarizing" strategy to their students and work toward mastery on that, grade four teachers should be able to assume some degree of competence with this question and will only need to review, rather than teach (or reteach) it. They can then focus on teaching a few additional text responses, so that the response repertoire of students will continue to expand.

Below are some guidelines for designing a written response curriculum.

Guidelines for Designing a Written Response Curriculum Grades 2-8

1. **Select a reasonable number of questions for any given grade.** The goal is to get students to achieve *independence*, so it is unrealistic to identify too many questions at each grade level. How many questions can teachers and students manage comfortably in one year? If you're serious about making this a *comprehensive* plan, you would need a minimum of four questions. Unless you have few other important curricular priorities, it's unrealistic to expect a grade-level teacher to cover more than six text responses.

2. **Select questions in all three thinking strands (Constructing Basic Meaning, Analyzing the Text, and Text Plus) for study in each grade.** Regardless of grade level, students need to engage in different kinds of thinking. It's tempting to focus only on literal questions in the lower grades, because these are easier than questions that ask students to interpret or extend the meaning of the text. However, even primary grade children

can think deeply about their reading, given questions to which they can make personal connections. For instance, they may have difficulty relating to the abstract concept of "theme," but could more easily identify what a character "cared about" based on events that transpired in a story.

3. **Provide for some introductory work on text response in the primary grades.** In kindergarten and first-grade, text response should be oral, not written. In these grades the goal is to expose young children to the language of response. This helps them understand that you can respond to a question systematically, and that good responses are accurate and thorough. Second grade is not too soon to get specific with questions related to text elements (I.A.). Some students may be able to respond to text element questions in writing using the answer organizers and frames provided. For others, you may want to modify the expectations with more basic graphic supports.

4. **Select questions that tap different areas of literary analysis.** For example, questions III.D and III.I both ask students to predict. During a given year, select just one of those questions, and substitute another question that focuses on character development, author's craft, or some other dimension of text study.

5. **Monitor students' growth over time.** For this instruction to work, teachers not only have to use it, they have to use it well. That means honoring all phases of explicit instruction initially, and providing for sufficient practice as follow-up until students reach independence. One easy technique for monitoring improved performance is to select a few students from a classroom (at different learning levels) and watch their growth over time. How did student "A" do after one lesson? After two lessons? After five lessons? How long did it take her to get to independence (responding without the assistance of a graphic organizer or frame)? How did her performance compare to that of a student who learns more quickly? Less quickly?

The following Scope and Sequence adheres to these guidelines. It may be customized to meet the needs of your school or district.

Scope and Sequence for Teaching Written Response to Text, Grades 2-8

Grade 2

I.A   According to this text, [who / what / when / where / how]
_____? Why is this important?

Grade 3

I.C   What is the problem or conflict in this text? Give specific details to support your answer.

I.E   How does [character / person] solve his or her problem in this text?

I.D   Briefly summarize what happens in this story.

III.C List _____ questions you would like to ask the author that are not answered in this text. Explain why you would like an answer to each question.

II.K   How can you tell that [character / author / person] cared about _____?

Grade 4

I.H   If you could rename this [story / article / chapter] what would you call it?

I.B   Choose one word that best describes [name of character / important person] and provide evidence from the text to support your choice.

II.D   What lesson can we learn from the [article / story / chapter]?

II.C   What details in the text support the conclusion that _____?

III.B What might [character / person] have written in his/her journal after this event happened in the text: _____?

Grade 5

I.G   What would you say is the main idea of this [article / chapter / paragraph]?

II.B   What is the purpose of this [paragraph / line] on page _____?

II.E   Choose a [line / paragraph] from this text that you consider to be very important. Why do you think it is important?

III.I What do you think will happen next? Use information from the text to support your answer.

II.J   Find one fact and one opinion in this [article / chapter / story]. How do you know whether it is a fact or an opinion?

Grade 6

II.H From whose point of view is this text written? Why do you think the author chose this voice?

III.D Based on information in this text, what probably would have happened if _____?

III.J Imagine that you are giving a talk to your class about _____. Using information from the text, write two ideas you would use in your speech.

III.H Does something in this text remind you of something in your own life? Explain or describe.

III.E Using information from this text, how do you visualize this scene?

Grade 7

III.A How is this text similar to another text you read?

II.I What is the structure/organization of this text? Why do you think the author chose this structure?

II.G What is one author's craft technique found in this text that makes the writing lively? Give examples.

III.G If you had been [person / character] how would you have handled the situation when _____?

Grade 8

III.H How is [someone or something described in this text] similar to someone or something in our world today?

II.F Do you consider this text to be 'good' literature? Why or why not?

The remainder of this book provides classroom-ready materials to help you to truly teach written response to text. May it offer just what you need to do that job well.

PART TWO

Instructional Supports

QUESTION I.A

According to this text, [who / what/ when / where / why/ how] _____? Why is this important?

PLEASE ANSWER THIS QUESTION FOR THE FOLLOWING TEXT:_____

WHAT YOU NEED TO DO:

1. Write a topic sentence that answers who / what / when / where / why / how.

2. Write one or more sentences that explain why this is important to this story or situation.

3. Write one or more sentences that tell one <u>important</u> outcome or event that happened because of this.

I.A According to this text, [who / what / when / where / how]_____. Why is this important?

THE NARRATIVE MODEL
Based on the story *Lily's Crossing* by Patricia Reilly Giff

The question:
Where and when does the story *Lily's Crossing* take place, and why is this setting important to the story?

The answer:

Lily's Crossing takes place in a town called Rockaway during the summer of 1944. This town is right on the ocean which is very important because many events of the story are connected to the ocean. The time is important because it is during World War II. Many of the story's events take place because Lily's father has gone to Europe to fight in the war, and Albert has come from Hungary because the Nazis killed his parents. The most important event involving this setting is that Lily (the main character) teaches her new friend, Albert, to swim, and then Albert almost drowns one night when he is trying to swim out to a ship bound for Europe, so he can rescue his little sister.

I.A According to this text, [who / what / when / where / how]_____. Why is this important?

THE EXPOSITORY MODEL
Based on an article in *Thomas Edison*, an issue of *Kids Discover* Magazine

The question:
How did Thomas Edison figure out how to make the electric light bulb and why was this such an important invention?

The answer:

    The way Thomas Edison came up with his light bulb was he knew he needed a thread that would glow for a long time without burning up, and a container that had almost no air in it. He kept experimenting until he figured out the right combination of materials. This was an important invention because for the first time people could light their houses with electricity which was better and safer than kerosene and gas lamps. If the light bulb had not been invented our life would be very different today.

I.A According to this text, [who / what / when / where / how]_____. Why is this important?

ANSWER ORGANIZER

1. Write a sentence that tells who / what / when / where / why / how.

   _____

   _____

   _____

2. Write one or more sentences that tell why this is important to the story or situation.

   _____

   _____

   _____

   _____

3. Write one or more sentences that tell about something big that happens because of this.

   _____

   _____

   _____

   _____

I.A   **According to this text, [who / what / when / where / how]_____. Why is this important?**

ANSWER FRAME for "where" and "when" (setting)

This story / event takes place _____

_____. The time is _____

_____. This place and time are

important because_____

_____

_____

_____.

Something big that happens because of this setting is _____

_____

_____

_____.

I.A **According to this text, [who / what / when / where / how]_____. Why is this important?**

ANSWER FRAME for "who" (person / character)

The person / character this is mostly about is _____

_____. He or she is important to what happens

because_____

_____

_____. If it hadn't been for this

person / character _____

_____

_____.

I.A According to this text, [who / what / when / where / how]_____. **Why is this important?**

ANSWER FRAME for "what"

What happens in this part of the reading is _____
_____
_____.

This is important because_____
_____
_____.

Something big that happens because of this is _____
_____
_____.

I.A   **According to this text, [who / what / when / where / how]_____. Why is this important?**

ANSWER FRAME for "why"

This event happened because_____

_____

_____.

This event is important to this story or situation because

_____

_____

_____.

As a result of this _____

_____

_____.

I.A   **According to this text, [who / what / when / where / how]_____. Why is this important?**

ANSWER FRAME for "how"

The way this happened was _____

_____

_____ .

This was important to this story or situation because

_____

_____ .

Something important that happened because of this is

_____

_____

QUESTION I.B

Choose one word that best describes [name of character / person] (kind, friendly, lazy, responsible, etc.) and provide evidence from the text to support your choice.

PLEASE ANSWER THIS QUESTION FOR THE FOLLOWING TEXT:_____

WHAT YOU NEED TO DO:

1. Write a topic sentence that includes the name of the character or person and his or her important trait.

2. Write two or three specific things that happened in the text where the character or person showed this trait. (You will need 3-5 sentences to do this.)

3. Use a quote from the text that proves this trait with the author's own words.

I.B Choose one word that best describes [name of character / person] (kind, friendly, lazy, responsible, etc.) and provide evidence from the text to support your choice.

THE NARRATIVE MODEL
Based on the story *Pink and Say* by Patricia Polacco

The question:
Choose one word that best describes Pink (kind, friendly, lazy, responsible, etc.) and provide evidence from the text that supports your choice.

The answer:

One word that really describes Pink is *caring*. He showed this many times in this story. First he cared about Say when he was wounded and he carried him all the way back to his house. He also cared about his country. He fought with the Forty-eighth Colored in the Civil War, trying to win freedom for slaves. Third, Pink really cared about his mother. He said he and Say should leave his house because they were putting his mother in danger. But then marauders attacked and killed his mom. The story says, " 'Your son loves you, Moe Moe Bay. Your son loves you.' He sobbed as he held her."

I.B Choose one word that best describes [name of character / person] (kind, friendly, lazy, responsible, etc.) and provide evidence from the text to support your choice.

THE EXPOSITORY MODEL
Based on *Thomas Edison*, an issue of *Kids Discover*

The question:
Choose one word that best describes Thomas Edison (kind, friendly, lazy, responsible, etc.) and provide evidence from the text to support your choice.

The answer:

I think the word "curious" really describes Thomas Edison. Even as a young boy he was curious. One time when he was little, he sat on goose eggs because he wondered if he could get them to hatch. When he got older he experimented with lots of things and that's how he got to be a famous inventor. For example he invented a vote recorder, a phonograph, and even a talking doll. His most famous invention is the kind of electric lightbulb that people could use in their homes. On page 6 it says, "Early in his life, Edison showed the inquisitive mind of a scientist."

I.B Choose one word that best describes [name of character / person] (kind, friendly, lazy, responsible, etc.) and provide evidence from the text to support your choice.

ANSWER ORGANIZER

1. Write a topic sentence that includes the name of the character or person and his/her important trait.

   _____

   _____

2. Write one or two sentences about one event in the text that shows this trait.

   _____

   _____

3. Write one or two sentences about a second event that shows this trait.

   _____

   _____

4. Write one or two sentences about a third event that shows this trait. (You can skip this part if you can't find another example.)

   _____

   _____

5. Write a sentence with a quote from the text that proves this trait in the author's own words.

   _____

   _____

I.B Choose one word that best describes [name of character / person] (kind, friendly, lazy, responsible, etc.) and provide evidence from the text to support your choice.

ANSWER FRAME

One word that really describes_____

is _____. One time s/he showed this was when

_____

_____

Another time s/he showed this was when _____

_____

_____

A third time s/he showed this was when _____

_____

_____.

Here's a quote from the author that proves that this

character/person was very _____: "_____

_____

_____."

QUESTION I.C

What is the problem or conflict in this text? Give specific details to support your answer.

PLEASE ANSWER THIS QUESTION FOR THE FOLLOWING TEXT:_____

WHAT YOU NEED TO DO:

1. Write a topic sentence that tells the problem that gets the story or situation going.

2. Write a sentence that gives an important detail about this problem.

3. Write a sentence with a quote from the text that shows evidence of this problem.

4. If there is more than one part to the problem, give another detail and find a quote as evidence.

5. Write a concluding sentence that says why this problem needed to be solved.

I.C   What is the problem or conflict in this text? Give specific details to support your answer.

THE NARRATIVE MODEL
Based on the story *Shiloh* by Phyllis Reynolds Nailor

The question:
What is the problem at the beginning of *Shiloh* that gets the story going? Give specific details from the story to support your answer.

The answer:

   The problem at the beginning of *Shiloh* is that Marty wants to keep Shiloh for himself even though the dog belongs to Judd Travers. Also, his parents say he can't have a pet. Marty wants Shiloh because Judd is so mean to his dogs. Judd says, "When I want 'em I whistle; when I don't I give 'em a kick." Marty's mom won't let him get a pet because they are too poor. She said, "If you can't afford to feed 'em and take 'em to the vet when they're sick, you've no right taking 'em in." For the rest of the story Marty tries to figure out how to get Shiloh for his very own dog.

THE EXPOSITORY MODEL
Based on "Jim Crow" in *The Day Martin Luther King, Jr., Was Shot* by Jim Haskins

The question:
What new problem did African-Americans who remained in the South face after Reconstruction? Give specific details from the text to support your answer.

The answer:

After Reconstruction of the South was over, African-Americans had to face a new problem, the Jim Crow laws. These laws were made up to keep blacks and whites separate in almost every area of life. In some southern towns there were actually laws that "prevented blacks and whites from playing checkers together in public or looking out the same factory window at the same time." Even though these laws really discriminated against black people, the Supreme Court said "separate but equal" was not against the law. This problem needed to be solved because it meant black people still didn't have the freedom they deserved.

I.C **What is the problem or conflict in this text? Give specific details to support your answer.**

ANSWER ORGANIZER

1. Write a topic sentence that tells the problem that gets the story or situation going.

   _____

   _____

2. Write one detail that tells something important about this problem.

   _____

   _____

3. Write a quote from the text that shows how bad this problem is.

   _____

   _____

4. If there is another important part of the problem, write it here. (If not, skip to step #5.)

   _____

   _____

   _____

5. Write a final sentence that says why this problem needed to be solved.

   _____

   _____

I.C **What is the problem or conflict in this text? Give specific details to support your answer.**

ANSWER FRAME (for one-part problem)

The main problem that gets this story or situation going

is_____

_____. Something important about his problem

is_____

_____.

Here is a quote that shows how bad this problem is:_____

_____

_____

It was really important to solve this problem because_____

_____

_____

I.C **What is the problem or conflict in this text? Give specific details to support your answer.**

ANSWER FRAME (for two-part problem)

The main problem that gets this story or situation going

is_____

_____. Something important about his problem

is_____

_____

_____.

Here is a quote that shows how bad this problem is:_____

_____

_____

Something else very important about this problem is _____

_____

_____.

Here is a quote that proves this is a bad problem:_____

_____

_____.

After this, _____ tries really hard to solve this problem

because_____.

QUESTION I.D

Briefly summarize what happens in this story.

PLEASE ANSWER THIS QUESTION FOR THE FOLLOWING STORY:_____

WHAT YOU NEED TO DO:

1. Write a topic sentence that includes the name of the main character, where the story takes place, and the problem that gets the action going. (If this takes more than one sentence, that's okay.)

2. Write three specific *important* things that happen in the story. (This may be one long sentence or three short sentences.)

3. Write a sentence that tells what happens in the story to solve the problem.

4. Tell how the story ends.

©2002 Nancy N. Boyles, Teaching Written Response

THE NARRATIVE MODEL
Based on the fable "The Bad Kangaroo" in *Fables* by Arnold Lobel

The question:
Briefly summarize what happens in the fable "The Bad Kangaroo."

The answer:

This fable is about a little kangaroo who was so bad in school that the principal went to his house to tell his parents about his behavior. As soon as he got there the parents started doing things like putting a thumbtack on the principal's chair, throwing spit balls, and sticking glue on the doorknobs. In the end, the principal ran out of the house and the parents couldn't figure out why he left.

ANSWER ORGANIZER

1. Write one or more sentences that include the name of the main character, where the story takes place, and the problem that gets the action going.

    _____

    _____

    _____

2. Write a sentence that tells one important thing that happens in the story.

    _____

    _____

3. Write a sentence that tells a second important thing that happens in the story.

    _____

    _____

4. Write a sentence that tells a third important thing that happens in the story.

    _____

    _____

5. Write a sentence that tells how the problem gets solved and how the story ends.

    _____

    _____

ANSWER FRAME

   This story is about a main character named _____

and takes place _____. The problem that

gets the action going is _____

_____. One important

thing that happens as the characters try to solve this problem is

_____

_____.

A second important thing that happens in the story is _____

_____.

A third important thing that happens is _____

_____.

Finally the problem gets solved when _____

_____.

At the end of the story_____

_____.

QUESTION I.E

How does [the main character / important person] solve his/her problem in this text?

PLEASE ANSWER THIS QUESTION FOR THE FOLLOWING TEXT:_____

WHAT YOU NEED TO DO:

1. In one sentence tell briefly what the main character or person does to solve his or her problem.

2. Write two or three sentences that give some of the details about how the problem gets solved.

3. Write a sentence that tells how the characters or people feel when the problem has been solved.

4. Try to find a quote from the text to prove that what you're saying about the solution is really true.

THE NARRATIVE MODEL
Based on *Shiloh* by Phyllis Reynolds Naylor

The question:

In the story *Shiloh*, how does Marty solve his problem?

The answer:

In the story *Shiloh*, Marty solves his problem of wanting to keep Shiloh for his very own dog by making a deal with Judd. He sees Judd shoot a deer when it isn't even hunting season and tells Judd he is going to report him. Judd knows he will be in big trouble for breaking the law, so he agrees to let Marty keep the dog if he can pay him $40, which is what the dog cost him to buy. By now Marty's parents love Shiloh, too, so they say he can have Shiloh. At the end Marty's whole family is happy. The story says, "Ma's baked a chocolate cake to celebrate—a real cake, too, not no Betty Crocker."

THE EXPOSITORY MODEL
Based on the chapter "Coming Over" from *Immigrant Kids* by Russell Freedman

The question:
In the chapter "Coming Over," how is Angelo Pellegrini's family finally allowed to enter the United States from Ellis Island?

The answer:

Angelo's family was finally allowed to enter the United States because his mother convinced the doctor that her little girl was not sick. At first the officials would not let his family in because they thought the little girl's red eyes meant she was sick. It looked like they might have to go back to Italy. But the mother convinced them. She said that her child's eyes were bloodshot because she'd been crying so much. If she had a few hours' rest and something to eat, she would be all right. In the end, the family was happy because they could stay in America. It's a good thing that Mother was "an indomitable spirit."

ANSWER ORGANIZER

1. Write a sentence that tells the problem in the story or situation and then briefly explain how the character or person solves this problem.

    _____

    _____

2. Write two or three sentences with <u>details</u> about how this problem gets solved.

    _____

    _____

    _____

    _____

    _____

3. Write a sentence that explains how the characters or people feel when the problem has been solved.

    _____

    _____

4. Try to find a quote that supports what you're saying about the solution of the problem.

    _____

    _____

ANSWER FRAME

_____ solves the problem of _____
(Character's/person's name)

_____by_____

_____.

S/he does this by _____

_____

_____.

Here is how the story or situation ends:_____

_____.

This makes _____ feel very _____
(character/person)

because_____

_____.

QUESTION I.F

What was your first reaction to this text? Please explain using specific examples.

PLEASE ANSWER THIS QUESTION FOR THE FOLLOWING TEXT:_____

WHAT YOU NEED TO DO:

1. Write a topic sentence that tells your first reaction to this text. (This might be a *feeling* or a question, or something the text made you *think about*.)

2. Try to think of two or three *details* from the text related to this feeling, question, or thought and write a sentence about each one. Be sure to elaborate on each detail.

3. Write a summary sentence to tie your details together.

THE NARRATIVE MODEL
Based on the story *Faithful Elephants: A True Story of Animals, People and War* by Yukio Tsuchiya

The question:
What was your first reaction to the story *Faithful Elephants*? Why did you react this way?

The answer:

My first reaction to this story was that I felt horrified. First of all, I was horrified because three elephants died. Since I love animals I can't stand thinking that they were in pain, or even worse, starved to death. I was also horrified because I never thought about war being bad for animals. Like the story says, 'What would happen if bombs hit the zoo?" I never considered before that wild animals might escape and run into the streets. Another reason I was horrified was that I always thought of Japan as being bad in the war. But these zoo workers didn't look like bad people and they loved their animals. This story made me think about how horrible war is for all living things.

THE EXPOSITORY MODEL
Based on "School Days" in *Ancient Egypt*, an issue of *Appleseeds*

The question:
What was your first reaction to the article "School Days?"
Why did you react this way?

The answer:

My first reaction was that I was surprised because this article says that most Egyptian children did not go to school and they did not learn to read and write. This was surprising to me because today in our country there is a law that children have to go to school, and reading and writing are not that hard. In Egypt, only the smartest children went to scribal school, and most were boys. Learning to read and write took a long time. The article says, "It took years to learn how to write the hundreds of signs called *hieroglyphs*." That sounds very complicated to me. I would not want to be a child in ancient Egypt.

ANSWER ORGANIZER

1. Write a topic sentence telling your first reaction to this story or situation. (It might be a feeling, a question, or a thought you had while reading.)

    _____

    _____

2. Write one detail about the story or situation related to this feeling, question, or wondering.

    _____

    _____

    _____

3. Write a second detail about the story or situation related to this feeling, question, or wondering.

    _____

    _____

    _____

4. If you can think of a third detail, write about it here.

    _____

    _____

    _____

5. Write a final sentence tying your details together.

    _____

    _____

I.F   **What was your first reaction to this [story / chapter / article]? Why did you react this way?**

ANSWER FRAME

My first reaction to this story or situation was _____

_____. One

reason I reacted this way was _____

_____

_____.

A second reason I reacted this way was _____

_____

_____.

A third reason I reacted this way was _____

_____

_____.

For these reasons the story or situation made me realize that

_____

_____.

QUESTION 1.G

What would you say is the main idea of this text?

PLEASE ANSWER THIS QUESTION FOR THE FOLLOWING TEXT:_____

WHAT YOU NEED TO DO:

1. Write a topic sentence that states the main idea.

2. Write one sentence that explains how you know this is the main idea.

3. Give two or three details from the text that support this main idea. It would be good to use some of the author's exact words. (2 or 3 sentences)

THE NARRATIVE MODEL
Based on the story *Lily's Crossing* by Patricia Reilly Giff

The question:
What is the main idea of the third paragraph of Chapter 15 that begins, "Now she took the letters and went straight to Margaret's house..."

The answer:
The main idea of this paragraph is that Lily really wants to take the time to enjoy these letters all by herself. I can tell this because all the details in the paragraph are about this. First, she took the letters to Margaret's room where could be all alone. Then the author says that she had "time, plenty of time." Last of all, Lily compared reading her letters to sucking on a red lifesaver that melts slowly. I think she wanted this special moment to last and last like the lifesaver.

THE EXPOSITORY MODEL
**Based on *We Came to North America: The Africans* by
Jen Green**

The question:
What is the main idea of paragraph 2 on page 14?

The answer:

    The main idea of this paragraph is that seeing North America for the first time was terrifying for the African slaves. I can tell this is the main idea because all of the rest of the sentences in this paragraph are details about why this was so terrifying. For example the author says, "The cities were strange and filled with oddly dressed white people." This paragraph also says that no one spoke the Africans' language and that they were examined like animals and sold as slaves.

ANSWER ORGANIZER

1. Write a topic sentence that states the main idea.

   _____

   _____

2. Write a sentence that explains how you know this is the main idea.

   _____

   _____

3. Write one detail that shows that this is the main idea. Try to use some of the author's exact words.

   _____

   _____

4. Write a second detail that shows that this is the main idea. Try to use some of the author's exact words.

   _____

   _____

5. For an extra-strong answer, write about a third detail, with some of the author's exact words.

   _____

   _____

ANSWER FRAME

The main idea of this is _____

_____.

I can tell this is the main idea because _____

_____.

Some details that support this are:

1._____

_____.

2._____

_____

3._____

_____.

Question I.H

If you could rename this [story / article / chapter], what would you call it and why?

PLEASE ANSWER THIS QUESTION FOR THE FOLLOWING STORY: _____

WHAT YOU NEED TO DO:

1. Write a topic sentence that states the new title you would choose for this text.

2. Write about three sentences that explain why this would be a good title based on what happens in this text.

3. Choose a quote from the text that proves what you are saying.

4. Write a final "As you can see. . ." sentence that says your new title would be a good one for this text.

THE NARRATIVE MODEL
Based on "Your Name in Gold" by A.F. Bauman in *Chicken Soup for the Kid's Soul*

The question:
If you could choose a new title for "Your Name in Gold," what title would you choose, and why?

The answer:
If I could rename this story I would call it "The Argument." I think this would be a good title because these two sisters, Anne and Mary, both want to send away for the same prize from a cereal box. First Mary says she should get it because she saw it first, and she has the money to buy it. Anne begs her sister because she wants the prize really badly. Then she stomps out of the room, crying. She yells, "Just go ahead and send in for it. See if I care!". As you can see, these sisters are having a bad argument. But it gets solved in the end.

THE EXPOSITORY MODEL
Based on *Dinner at Aunt Connie's House* by Faith Ringgold

The question:
If you could choose a new title for *Dinner at Aunt Connie's House*, what would you call it, and why?

The answer:

If I could choose a different title for *Dinner at Aunt Connie's House*, I would call it "The Magical Paintings." I think this would be a good title because the pictures of famous African-American women in Aunt Connie's attic all came to life and talked to the children. The first painting to come to life was a picture of Rosa Parks, and she talked about getting arrested for refusing to sit in the back of the bus. Some other paintings also came to life, like Mary McLeod Bethune and Bessie Smith. Bessie said, "I inspired many singers with my soul and spirit." As you can see, these paintings really were magical.

ANSWER ORGANIZER

1.   Write a topic sentence that states the new title you would choose for this text.

_____

_____

2.   Write about three or four sentences that explain why this would be a good title based on what happens in the text.

_____

_____

_____

_____

_____

_____

3.   Choose a quote from the text that proves what you are saying.

_____

_____

_____

4.   Write a final "As you can see. . ." sentence that says your new title would be a good one for this text.

_____

_____

ANSWER FRAME

If I could choose a different title for this text it would be

_____.

I think this would be a good title because of what happens in this

text. Here is what happens: _____

_____

_____

_____

_____.

Here is a quote from the text that proves what I am saying:

_____

_____

_____.

As you can see, _____

would be another good title for this text!

QUESTION II.A

How did [character / person] change from the beginning of the text to the end of the text?

PLEASE ANSWER THIS QUESTION FOR THE FOLLOWING TEXT:_____

WHAT YOU NEED TO DO *BEFORE* YOU WRITE:

1. Think about *one* important way the character changed. (Did his/her *thinking* change? Did his/her *actions* change?)

WHAT YOU NEED TO DO *WHEN* YOU WRITE:

1. Write a topic sentence that tells how the character acts or thinks at the *beginning* of the text.

2. Give an example from the text that really shows this character trait. (One or more sentences)

3. Tell about an event from the text that causes the character to change. (One or more sentences)

4. In one sentence, tell how the character acts or thinks at the end of the text.

5. Find a quote from the text that proves this change.

II.A How did [character / person] change from the beginning of the text to the end of the text?

THE NARRATIVE MODEL
Based on the story *Lily's Crossing* by Patricia Reilly Giff

The question:
How did Lily change from the beginning of the story to the end of the story?

The answer:

At the beginning of this story Lily has a problem with lying. Her worst lie is that she tells her friend Albert that she is going to swim out of their harbor to an aircraft carrier or destroyer that is on its way to Europe to win the war against the Nazis. She says she is going to climb aboard and find her father somewhere in Europe. Of course she knows she could never do this, but Albert doesn't realize she is lying. One night he tries to row out to meet a ship so he can get back to his sister in France. There is a big storm. He nearly drowns because he can't swim. After this close call, Lily doesn't lie anymore. The story says, "Every time she started to lie, she thought of Albert and closed her mouth."

ANSWER ORGANIZER

1. Write a topic sentence that tells how the character or person acts or thinks at first.

    _____

    _____

2. Give an example that shows this character trait.

    _____

    _____

    _____

3. Tell about the event that causes the character or person to change.

    _____

    _____

    _____

4. Tell how the character or person acts or thinks at the end, and give an example.

    _____

    _____

    _____

5. Write a quote from the story that proves this change.

    _____

    _____

II.A **How did [character / person] change from the beginning of the text to the end of the text?**

ANSWER FRAME

At the beginning of this story, _____ shows by

his or her actions or behavior that_____

_____.

S/he shows this when _____

_____.

Then something big happens that causes this behavior to change.

Here's what happens:_____

_____

_____.

At the end of the story [character]_____

now shows that _____

_____.

Here is a quote from the story that proves this change:

_____

_____.

QUESTION II.B

What is the purpose of this [paragraph / line] on page ___?

PLEASE ANSWER THIS QUESTION FOR THE FOLLOWING TEXT:_____

WHAT YOU NEED TO DO:

1. Write a topic sentence that tells *why* you think the author included this paragraph or line. (Maybe the author wrote it to describe something, to show a character trait, to build suspense, provide information, introduce an idea — or for some other reason.)

2. Give some details about the paragraph or line so the person reading your answer will understand who the characters or people are, what the scene or situation is about, or why the description is importanr. (About two sentences)

3. Explain how this paragraph or line is related to something else important that happens in the text. (One or two sentences)

4. Write an "As you can see..." sentence that restates your topic sentence.

THE NARRATIVE MODEL
Based on the story *Mississippi Bridge* by Mildred D. Taylor

The question:

What is the purpose of this paragraph on page 15:
> "Hat like that sure 'nough would put a little sunshine in this gloom," said Mr. Wallace. "Why don't you go 'head try it on, Miz Hattie? It sure would set well on your fine head of hair."

The answer:

I think the author wrote this paragraph to show that there was a lot of discrimination against black people in Mississippi in the 1930s. Mr. Wallace was a shopkeeper and in this paragraph he was telling one of his customers (a rich white lady) she could try on a hat, hoping she would buy it. This is important because right before this, Mr. Wallace treated a poor black customer very differently. He wouldn't let her try on the hat before she bought it, and she couldn't even exchange it after she put it on her head. As you can see, Mr. Wallace was much nicer to the lady with white skin.

THE EXPOSITORY MODEL
Based on *The Heart: Our Circulatory System* by Seymour Simon

The question:
What is the purpose of this paragraph on page 1?"
> "Make a fist. This is about the size of your heart. Sixty to one hundred times every minute your heart muscles squeeze together and push blood around your body through tubes called blood vessels."

The answer:

I think the purpose of this paragraph is to introduce this book about the heart in a way that gets the reader's attention. When the author tells me to make a fist, that gets my attention because I tried it out and now I want to see how something that size could do so much work. It also says that the job of the heart is to push blood around your body. This is important because it helps me predict that the rest of the book will probably explain how the heart really works. As you can see, this paragraph is a good introduction to this book.

ANSWER ORGANIZER

1. Write a topic sentence that tells why you think the author included this paragraph or line.

    _____

    _____

    _____

2. Give some details about this line or paragraph to explain what is going on in this part of the text. (What are these lines saying about a character or event?)

    _____

    _____

    _____

    _____

3. Explain why this paragraph or line is important to the text. (How does it fit in with what comes before or after it?)

    _____

    _____

    _____

4. Write an "As you can see" sentence that tells again the purpose of this paragraph or line.

    _____

    _____

ANSWER FRAME

I think the author included this paragraph/line to show that

_____

_____. Here are some

details about this part of the text: _____

_____

_____

_____

This paragraph/line is important to the text because _____

_____

_____

_____

As you can see, this shows that the purpose of this line/paragraph

is to: _____

_____.

©2002 Nancy N. Boyles, Teaching Written Response

QUESTION II.C

What details in the text support the conclusion that
_____**?**

PLEASE ANSWER THIS QUESTION FOR THE FOLLOWING TEXT:_____

WHAT YOU NEED TO DO:

1. Write a topic sentence that states the conclusion identified in the question above.

2. Tell two or three details from the text that support this conclusion. Include a quote about at least one of these details.

3. Write a final sentence that shows why these details were important.

THE NARRATIVE MODEL
Based on the story *Letters from Rifka* by Karen Hesse

The question:
What details from the story support the conclusion that Rifka was "clever"? Why was being clever important to Rifka?

The answer:

Many times during this story Rifka proved that she was very clever. At the beginning of the book she figured out how to distract some guards at the train station so they wouldn't search for her family who was escaping from Russia. She did this by starting a big conversation with them so they wouldn't have time to ask her questions. Also, Rifka proved she was clever because she learned to speak many languages very quickly, and this helped her communicate. When she was in Poland and Belgium she learned the languages of those countries. Then while she was stuck in a hospital at Ellis Island, she learned to read and write English in only three weeks. Being clever really helped Rifka to survive.

THE EXPOSITORY MODEL
Based on the book *Welcome to the Green House*, by Jane Yolen

The question:
What details from this text support the conclusion that a tropical rainforest is a lot like a house? Why is this important?

The answer:

A tropical rainforest is a lot like a house because of the way it is built, and also because it has lots of inhabitants, and sometimes they are noisy. For example, a rainforest doesn't have real windows, but it does have "ropey vines that frame the views." It is filled with all sorts of creatures like monkeys, snakes, birds, lizards, and fish. It is also very noisy. One sound is the "crinch-crunch of long-horned beetles chewing through wood." It is important to think of a tropical rainforest as a house with lots of life in it because then we might try harder to protect it.

ANSWER ORGANIZER

1. What is the conclusion identified in this question? Write a sentence that states this conclusion _____

    _____

    _____

2. Tell one detail from the text that supports this conclusion. You can add a quote for extra support.

    _____

    _____

    _____

3. Tell a second detail that supports this conclusion, perhaps adding a quote.

    _____

    _____

    _____

4. Tell a third detail if you can think of one.

    _____

    _____

    _____

5. Write a final sentence that shows why these details were important.

    _____

    _____

ANSWER FRAME

Lots of details in this text support the conclusion that

_____. One detail

that proves this was _____

_____

_____

Here is a quote from the text to prove this:_____

_____

_____

A second detail that supports this conclusion is _____

_____

_____.

To prove this, the text says, _____

_____

These details are important because_____

_____

_____.

QUESTION II.D

What lesson can we learn from this [article / story / chapter]?

PLEASE ANSWER THIS QUESTION FOR THE FOLLOWING TEXT:_____

WHAT YOU NEED TO DO:

1. Write a topic sentence that tells the message or lesson you think the author is trying to share.

2. Tell what happens at the beginning of the story or situation that shows that the characters or people have not learned this lesson yet. (Two or more sentences)

3. Tell what happens at the end of the story or situation that shows the characters or people have now learned this important lesson. (Two or more sentences)

4. Try to find a quote to prove that the lesson has been learned.

THE NARRATIVE MODEL
Based on the story *Frindle* by Andrew Clements

The question:
What message do you think the author wanted to share by writing the story *Frindle*?

The answer:

I think the author of *Frindle* was trying to show that when kids are creative in school and think for themselves, that teachers should be glad. At the beginning of this story, Mrs. Granger is really annoyed with Nick because he makes up a new word for *pen* — "frindle." Mrs. Granger thinks Nick is a troublemaker and wants him to stop this nonsense. However, soon people everywhere are saying "frindle" instead of "pen", and no one can stop this new word from spreading. At the end of the story (10 years later) when "frindle" gets added to the dictionary, Mrs. Granger admits she is proud of what Nick did. She said, "I now see that this is the kind of chance that a teacher hopes and dreams about — a chance to see bright young students take an idea they have learned in a boring old classroom and put it to a real test in their own world."

THE EXPOSITORY MODEL
Based on the book *Dinner at Aunt Connie's House* by Faith Ringgold

The question:
What message do you think the author wanted to share by writing this book?

The answer:

I think the author wanted to show that we can learn a lot about courage and hard work by looking at the lives of famous African-American women. At the beginning of this book the children didn't think that Aunt Connie's paintings of people like Rosa Parks and Sojourner Truth could talk to them. Then each painting came alive and the person told the story of her life. At the end, the children decide that Aunt Connie's paintings are a great inspiration and can have an effect on their own lives. Lonnie says, "When I grow up, I want to sing in opera houses all over the world. I know it will be hard, but not as hard for me as it was for Marian Anderson."

ANSWER ORGANIZER

1.   Write a topic sentence that tells the lesson or message you think the author wants to share.

   _____

   _____

2.   In two or more sentences, tell what happens at the beginning of the story or situation that shows that the characters or people have not learned this lesson yet.

   _____

   _____

   _____

   _____

3.   In two or more sentences, tell what happens at the end of the story that shows that the characters or people have now learned this lesson.

   _____

   _____

   _____

   _____

4.   Find a quote to prove that the lesson has been learned.

   _____

   _____

ANSWER FRAME

I think that by writing this the author wanted me to

understand that_____

_____.

At the beginning of the text I can tell that the characters or people

didn't understand this because_____

_____

_____

_____.

I can tell that the characters or people had learned this

lesson by the end of the text because_____

_____

_____

_____.

Here is a quote that proves that this lesson has been learned:

_____

_____

_____.

QUESTION II.E

Choose a line / paragraph from this text that you consider to be very important. Why do you think it is important?

PLEASE ANSWER THIS QUESTION FOR THE FOLLOWING TEXT:_____

WHAT YOU NEED TO DO:

1. Write a topic sentence that tells the line or paragraph of the text that you think is very important.

2. Give one or two reasons why you think this is a very important part. (Each reason will take one or two sentences.)

3. Try to find a quote that supports your answer.

THE NARRATIVE MODEL

Based on the story *Mississippi Bridge* by Mildred D. Taylor

The question:

Select a paragraph in *Mississippi Bridge* that you think is very important. Please explain your answer.

The answer:

I think a very important paragraph in *Mississippi Bridge* is on page 45 when the black people get off the bus so there will be room for the white people. I think this is very important for two reasons. First, it shows that the black people were scared of the bus driver and just did what he said without fighting back. The second reason is that the people who got off the bus were the ones who survived in the end when the bus skidded off the bridge and all the passengers drowned. It was surprising that the story would end like this with the black people living and the white people dying. Josias, a black boy in the story didn't understand this either. He said, "The Lord He work in mysterious ways."

II.E Choose a line / paragraph from this text that you consider to be very important. Why do you think it is important?

ANSWER ORGANIZER

1. Write a topic sentence that tells the paragraph or line of the text you think is very important.

    _____

    _____

2. Give one reason why you think this is very important part. (One or two sentences)

    _____

    _____

    _____

    _____

3. Think of a second reason why this part is important.

    _____

    _____

    _____

    _____

4. Find a quote to support your answer.

    _____

    _____

    _____

II.E   Choose a line / paragraph from this text that you consider to be very important. Why do you think it is important?

ANSWER FRAME

I think a very important part of this text is on page when

_____

_____.

I think this is important because_____

_____

_____.

Another reason I think this is important is because _____

_____

_____

_____.   Here is a quote that tells something

important about this part of the text:_____

_____

_____.

QUESTION II.F

Do you consider this text to be "good" literature? Why or why not?

PLEASE ANSWER THIS QUESTION FOR THE FOLLOWING STORY:_____

WHAT YOU NEED TO DO:

1. Look at the list of "Characteristics of Good Literature." Choose three characteristics from the list demonstrated in this text. (If you did *not* like the text, think of three characteristics that were *not* present.)

2. Write a topic sentence that says this text *is* or *is not* good literature based on three main reasons.

3. Write about each reason in one or two sentences. You should give exact details from the text about each reason.

4. Try to include a direct quote as evidence at least once in your answer.

5. Write a concluding sentence restating whether or not you think this text is *good* literature.

CHARACTERISTICS OF "GOOD" LITERATURE

Funny/Humorous

Scary

Full of feelings

Full of adventure and action

Shares an important message

Lots of description

Lots of interesting details

Believable characters

Relates to me

Surprise ending

OTHER REASONS FOR LIKING A STORY

_____

_____

_____

_____

_____

_____

THE NARRATIVE MODEL
Based on the story *Frindle* by Andrew Clements

The question:
Do you consider the story *Frindle* to be good literature? Why or why not?

The answer:
I think *Frindle* is good literature for three main reasons. First, it is very funny, and that made me want to keep reading. I love the way Nick does all kinds of wacky things, like he turns his classroom into a tropical island and spreads sand all over the floor. A second reason this is good literature is that the author makes the characters believable. At the beginning of the story it says, "Mrs. Granger didn't just enjoy the dictionary. She *loved* the dictionary — almost worshiped it." I could believe this because I once had a teacher like this. We used our dictionaries so much that mine was worn out by the end of the year. The final reason I think this is good literature is that it relates to me. I know how Nick feels when he gets blamed for something he didn't really do. That happens to me sometimes. These are all the reasons I think this story is good literature.

ANSWER ORGANIZER

1. Write a topic sentence that says that this text *is* or *is not* good literature based on three main reasons.

    _____
    _____

2. Name your first reason and give at least one detail from the text to support this. (You could add a quote for extra support.)

    _____
    _____
    _____
    _____

3. Name your second reason and give at least one detail from the text to support this. (You could add a quote for extra support.)

    _____
    _____
    _____
    _____

4. Name your third reason and give at least one detail from the text to support this. (You could add a quote for extra support.)

    _____
    _____

Continued next page

_____

_____

5. In one sentence, restate your opinion of this text.

_____

_____

ANSWER FRAME

I think this text is / is not good literature for three main

reasons. My first reason is that this text _____

_____.

You can see this in the text when _____

_____

_____.

The second reason I think this is / is not good literature is

_____.

Here is an example from the text that shows this: _____

_____

_____.

The third reason I think this is / is not good literature is

_____.

The text shows this when_____

_____.

Based on these three reasons I think this text is / is not an

example of good literature.

QUESTION II.G

What is one author's craft technique found in this text that makes the writing *lively*? Give examples.

PLEASE ANSWER THIS QUESTION FOR THE FOLLOWING TEXT:_____

WHAT YOU NEED TO DO:

1. Look at the list of craft techniques and choose one that really stands out to you in the text you read.

2. Look through the text and find two or three examples of this craft technique.

3. Write a topic sentence which includes the name of the craft technique that makes this writing lively.

4. For each example of the craft technique, do the following: (You can give each example its own paragraph.)
    a. Write the page number.
    b. Write a quote that contains the craft technique.
    c. Write a sentence that explains *how* this makes the writing lively.

5. Write a final sentence that names the craft technique again and says how it helped make the writing lively.

II.G What is one author's craft technique found in this text that makes the writing *lively?*
Give examples.

A FEW AUTHOR'S CRAFT TECHNIQUES

Precise nouns (including proper nouns)

Powerful verbs

Interesting adjectives

Dialogue that shows character traits

Figurative language

Alliteration

Similes and metaphors

Invented words

A good lead

A circular ending

A physical description

Anecdotes/examples

Instead of *said* (whispered, screamed, screeched, etc.)

Effective use of sentence fragments

Use of dashes and/or parentheses

Description that uses several of the senses

Concrete words

specific details that *show* rather than *tell*

A different point of view

An interesting way of organizing the story (like a journal or letter)

Character's private thoughts

Gesture

Facts

THE NARRATIVE MODEL
Based on the story *Missing May* by Cynthia Rylant

The question:
What is one craft technique that Cynthia Rylant uses in this story to make her writing lively?

The answer:

One craft technique that Cynthia Rylant uses in this story to make her writing lively is she uses similes to compare things. On page 5 she compares the old trailer where Ob and May lived to "a toy that God had been playing with and accidentally dropped out of heaven." This helps me picture the trailer as sort of run-down, but also a very loving place since it came from Heaven. Another simile I like is on page 22. "Cletus and Ob were as enthralled as cats in front of a fish tank" when they were doing a jigsaw puzzle. I can picture them really enjoying that puzzle. My favorite simile is on page 7 where Summer says, "I'd been treated like a homework assignment somebody was always having to do." I'd hate it if I got treated like a homework assignment. Cynthia Rylant's similes really help me picture things in my mind.

II.G What is one author's craft technique found in this text that makes the writing *lively*? Give examples.

THE EXPOSITORY MODEL

Based on the book, *Oh, Freedom!: Kids Talk about the Civil Rights Movement with the People who Made it Happen*, by Casey King and Linda Barrett Osborne

The question:

What is one craft technique the authors use in this book to make the writing lively?

The answer:

I think the writing in this book seems lively because of the structure that the authors used. It is set up with lots of interviews. Children interview adults who actually lived through segregation, so you find out first-hand what it was like to live in the South during this time. Here is one example from page 28:

Latoya: Well, what part of segregation do you remember the most?

Shirley: At one time, the buses were segregated. They had this little piece of wood, and this wood would be placed in some holes on the back of the seat. One side said, "For Coloreds Only." The other side said, "For Whites Only."

Continued next page

This writing seems lively because it is like a conversation and really shows feelings.

Here is another example of segregation that I found on page 62:

Bernard: (speaking to James Farmer): When did you first decide to do something about civil rights?

James: It was in Mississippi, when I was three and a half years old....I discovered I could not buy a Coca-Cola in a drugstore downtown even though a little white boy could.

I can picture James wanting that Coca-Cola so badly.

I think using interviews was a great way to write this book because you can picture what it was like to live in a segregated place.

ANSWER ORGANIZER

1. Write a topic sentence that includes the name of the craft technique that makes this writing lively.

    _____

    _____

2. Write one example of the craft technique including the page number and an exact quote.

    _____

    _____

    _____

3. Write a sentence that explains _how_ this makes the writing lively.

    _____

    _____

    _____

4. Write a second example of the craft technique including the page number and an exact quote.

    _____

    _____

    _____

Continued next page

II.G **What is one author's craft technique found in this text that makes the writing *lively*? Give examples. (Cont'd)**

5. Write a sentence that explains *how* this makes the writing lively.

   _____

   _____

   _____

6. You may want to write a third example of this craft technique including the page number and an exact quote.

   _____

   _____

   _____

7. Write a sentence that explains *how* this makes the writing lively.

   _____

   _____

   _____

8. If you found a third example, write a sentence that names this craft technique again and says *how* it helped make the writing lively.

   _____

   _____

II.G   What is one author's craft technique found in this text that makes the writing *lively*? Give examples.

ANSWER FRAME

One craft technique that helps make the writing in this text lively is _____.
There is an example of this on page _____ where the author says, "_____
_____." I think this makes the writing lively because_____
_____.

A second example of this craft technique is on page _____ where the author says, "_____
_____."
I think this makes the writing lively because_____
_____.

A third example of this technique is on page_____. The author says, "_____
_____." This helps make the writing lively because_____
_____.

The way the author uses _____ in this text really makes the writing lively by _____
_____.

QUESTION II.H

From whose point of view is this text written? Why do you think the author chose this voice? Give examples from the reading to support your answer.

PLEASE ANSWER THIS QUESTION FOR THE FOLLOWING TEXT:_____

WHAT YOU NEED TO DO:

1. Write a topic sentence that tells who the narrator is in this text.

2. Write a second sentence that explains why you think the author chose this voice.

3. Find a quote from the text as an example of this voice and explain why it makes the writing more effective. (One or two sentences)

4. If you can, find another quote and explain why it is effective. (One or two sentences)

5. Write a concluding sentence that tells why you like or do not like the voice used to narrate this text.

THE NARRATIVE MODEL
Based on the story *Shiloh* by Phyllis Reynolds Naylor

The question:
From whose point of view is this story written? Why do you think the author chose this voice? Give examples from the reading to support your answer.

The answer:

The narrator in this story is Marty. I think the author chose to write this from Marty's point of view because then you can really get to know his feelings. When Marty's dad tells him that Judd Travers wants to hunt on their land, the story says, "My whole body goes cold. I want to jump up and scream, 'No!' but I just grip my chair and wait it out." If Marty wasn't telling the story himself, you would not know how terrible he felt about this. Later in the story when Shiloh gets chewed up by another dog, the story says, "Hardest thing in the world is to leave Shiloh there at Doc. Murphy's, the way his eyes follow me." You can really tell how much Marty loves Shiloh. If someone else told this story, they couldn't know about these strong feelings.

THE EXPOSITORY MODEL
Based on *The Tree That Would Not Die* by Ellen Levine

The question:
From whose point of view is this text written? Why do you think the author chose this voice? Give examples from the reading to support your answer.

The answer:

This is written from the tree's point of view. Even though trees can't really talk, I think the author chose this voice because then you can compare the beauty of nature with the harm caused by people. This tree grew in Texas for a very long time. The story says, "I grew, but sometimes I didn't like what I saw. The First People and the settlers fought many battles." Then one day a stranger poisoned this old tree. "He crept into the park and poured a liquid in a circle by my side." Everyone thought the tree would die, but somehow, it survived. Hearing the tree tell its own story made me sad and angry because people were so mean. This was a good voice to use because maybe it will help people think more about their actions.

II.H From whose point of view is this text written? Why do you think the author chose this voice? Give examples from the reading to support your answer.

ANSWER ORGANIZER

1. Write a topic sentence that tells who the narrator is.

    _____

    _____

2. Write a sentence that tells why you think the author chose this voice.

    _____

    _____

3. Find a quote that shows how this voice makes the writing more effective. *How* does it make the writing effective?

    _____

    _____

    _____

4. If you can find a second good quote, write it and explain it here.

    _____

    _____

    _____

5. Write a final sentence that tells why you liked or didn't like the way the author used this voice.

    _____

    _____

II.H **From whose point of view is this text written? Why do you think the author chose this voice? Give examples from the reading to support your answer.**

ANSWER FRAME

The narrator in this text is _____.

I think the author chose this voice because_____

_____

_____. Here is a quote that shows this

voice:_____

_____.

This helps me understand that_____

_____.

Here is another quote that shows this voice:_____

_____

_____. It helps me understand that

_____.

I liked /didn't like the way the author used this voice because

_____

_____.

QUESTION II.I

What is the structure of this text? Why do you think the author chose this structure?

PLEASE ANSWER THIS QUESTION FOR THE FOLLOWING TEXT:_____

WHAT YOU NEED TO DO:

1. Write a topic sentence that tells the structure of the text? (It might be a narrative, a poem, a letter, a series of journal entries, etc.)

2. Write a sentence explaining why you think the author chose this structure.

3. Find and write a quote that shows this structure.

4. Write a sentence or two that tells what *you* like or do not like about this structure. (Does it make the writing more interesting or effective? Why?)

©2002 Nancy N. Boyles, Teaching Written Response

THE NARRATIVE MODEL
Based on *Letters from Rifka* by Karen Hesse

The question:
What is the structure of *Letters from Rifka*, and why do you think the author chose this structure?

The answer:

The story *Letters from Rifka* is written as a series of letters from Rifka to her cousin Tovah. I think the author chose this structure because writing to a cousin made the tone very personal. Also, the dates at the top of each letter let you know exactly when things were happening. This quote shows what I mean:

February 25, 1920
Antwerp, Belgium

Dear Tovah,
     Saying good-bye to Mama and Papa hurt in my chest
the way it hurt when Saul held me underwater too long.

I like this structure because I can see exactly when this event is happening, and I get to find out about Rifka's real feelings.

THE EXPOSITORY MODEL
Based on *Welcome to the Sea of Sand* by Jane Yolen

The question:
What is the structure of *Welcome to the Sea of Sand,* and why do you think the author chose this structure?

The answer:

   Welcome to the Sea of Sand is written as a poem. Lots of words rhyme and it sounds almost like a rap. I think Jane Yolen chose this structure because this book has a lot of information and you can remember it much better when the language has kind of a rhythm. Here is a quote that shows what I mean: "Welcome to the sand sea,

> all colors-of-the-band sea,
>
> a hot sea,
>
> a dry sea,
>
> a green-bush, red-rock, blue-sky sea."

I like this poem structure because it makes the desert sound really interesting. The poetry helps me get a good picture of these images in my mind.

ANSWER ORGANIZER

1. Write a topic sentence that names the structure of this text.

    _____

    _____

2. Write one or two sentences explaining why you think the author chose this structure.

    _____

    _____

    _____

3. Find and write a quote from the text to show this structure.

    _____

    _____

    _____

4. Write a final sentence that tells why you do or do not think this structure makes this text more effective.

    _____

    _____

    _____

ANSWER FRAME

This text is written as a _____

_____. I think the author chose this

structure because _____

_____

_____. Here is a quote that

shows this structure: _____

_____

_____.

I like / do not like this structure because _____

_____

_____.

QUESTION II.J

Choose one fact and one opinion in this text. How do you know that one is a fact, and the other is an opinion?

PLEASE ANSWER THIS QUESTION FOR THE FOLLOWING STORY:_____

WHAT YOU NEED TO DO:

1. Find one fact in the text (something that you can prove). Write a sentence that names this fact.

2. Write a sentence that explains how you know this is a fact. (Where can you find proof?)

3. Find an opinion in the text (something based on someone's point of view, something that someone else might disagree with, something you could <u>not</u> prove). Write a sentence that names this opinion.

4. Write a sentence that explains how you know this is an opinion. (Why can't this statement be proven true or false?)

Choose one fact and one opinion in this text. How do you know that one is a fact, and the other is an opinion?

THE NARRATIVE MODEL
Based on "Chapter One" from *26 Fairmont Avenue* by Tomie DePaola

The question:
Find one fact and one opinion in this chapter. How do you know that one is a fact, and the other is an opinion?

The answer:

One fact in this chapter is that in 1938 a big hurricane hit Meriden, Connecticut. I know this is a fact because the 1938 hurricane was very famous in New England and you can read about it in a lot of nonfiction books. One opinion is that Tomie says his best friend, Carol Crane, looked just like Shirley Temple. I think this is an opinion because you can't prove it. Some people might think this girl did not look like Shirley Temple.

11.1 Choose one fact and one opinion in this text. How do you know that one is a fact, and the other is an opinion?

THE EXPOSITORY MODEL
Based on the chapter "At Play" from *Immigrant Kids* by Russell Freedman

The question:
In the chapter "At Play," what is one fact and one opinion? How do you know that one is a fact, and the other is an opinion?

The answer:

One fact in this chapter is that kids played lots of games in the streets. I think this is a fact because there is a photograph on page 56 that shows this. One opinion is that the streets belonged to the children. Maybe the children felt like they owned the streets because they always played there. But that is really not a fact.

II.1 **Choose one fact and one opinion in this text. How do you know that one is a fact, and the other is an opinion?**

ANSWER ORGANIZER

1. Find one fact in the text (something that you can prove). Write a sentence that names this fact.

    _____

    _____

    _____

2. Write a sentence that explains how you know this is a fact. (Where can you find proof?)

    _____

    _____

    _____

3. Find an opinion in the text (something based on someone's point of view, something that someone else might disagree with, something you could <u>not</u> prove). Write a sentence that names this opinion.

    _____

    _____

    _____

4. Write a sentence that explains how you know this is an opinion. (Why can't this statement be proven true or false?)

    _____

    _____

    _____

II.I   Choose one fact and one opinion in this text. How do you know that one is a fact, and the other is an opinion?

ANSWER FRAME

One fact I found in this reading is _____

_____

_____.

I know this is a fact because _____

_____

_____.

An opinion that I found in this reading is _____

_____

_____.

I can tell this is an opinion because _____

_____

_____.

QUESTION II.K

How can you tell that [character / person / author] cared about _____**?**

PLEASE ANSWER THIS QUESTION FOR THE FOLLOWING STORY:_____

WHAT YOU NEED TO DO:

1. Write a topic sentence that says that the [character / person / author] cared about _____.

2. Write one or two sentence that show this caring using a detail from the text. (You may add a quote for extra support.)

3. Write about a second detail from the text that also shows this caring. (You may add a quote again for extra support.)

4. Write a "wrap-up" sentence that restates that the [character/person/author] cared about _____.

THE NARRATIVE MODEL
Based on "Bad News," a chapter in *School Spirit* by Johanna Hurwitz

The question:
How can you tell that Julio cares about his school?

The answer:

You can tell that Julio cares about his school because he wants to save it. One way I know this is because he is sad that his school might close. He says, "We don't want to go to another school. We like this one." Another way I know that Julio cares about his school is that he wants to try to change the school board's mind. He says, "Then it's up to us to make sure that they don't close the school." These actions and words show me that Julio really cares about his school.

THE EXPOSITORY MODEL
Based on *Satchmo's Blues* by Alan Schroeder

The question:
How can you tell that Louis Armstrong really cared about music?

The answer:

I can tell that Louis Armstrong really cared about music because every chance he got, he would stop and listen to jazz musicians playing their instruments. He wanted an instrument, too. He wanted "a real cornet, brass, with valves so quiet they whispered." He worked really hard to earn $5.00 so he could buy a horn he saw in a pawn shop. Then when he got his horn, he practiced and practiced until he could make beautiful music. He even became a world famous trumpeter. As you can see, Louis Armstrong really cared about music a lot.

ANSWER ORGANIZER

1. Write a topic sentence that says that the [character / person / author] cared about _____

    _____

    _____

2. Write one or two sentences that show this caring using a detail from the text. (You may add a quote for extra support.)

    _____

    _____

    _____

3. Write about a second detail from the text that also shows this caring. (You may add a quote again for extra support.)

    _____

    _____

    _____

4. Write a "wrap-up" sentence that restates that the [character/person/author] cared about

    _____

    _____

ANSWER FRAME

I can tell that _____ really cared

about _____ because _____

_____.

One detail from the text that shows this is _____

_____

_____.

A second detail from the text that shows this is _____

_____

_____.

I think these details show that _____ really cared

about _____.

QUESTION III.A

How is this text similar to another text you read?

PLEASE ANSWER THIS QUESTION FOR THE FOLLOWING STORY:_____

WHAT YOU NEED TO DO:

1. Think about another text that is like this one in some way. (Similar topic, character, problem, setting, message, etc.)

2. Write a topic sentence that names the two texts you are comparing and tells *how* they are similar.

3. Write a few sentences about this topic, message, feeling, etc. in the first book. Include a quote if possible.

4. Write a few sentences about the same topic, message, feeling, etc., in the second book. Include a quote if possible.

5. Write a final sentence or two about how this topic, message, feeling, etc., was important to both of these texts.

THE NARRATIVE MODEL
Based on the story *Missing May* by Cynthia Rylant

The question:
How is *Missing May* similar to another text you read?

The answer:

I think the story *Missing May* is similar to *Letters from Rifka* because both stories are about missing people. In *Missing May*, May dies at the beginning of the story. Her husband, Ob, misses her so much that once he couldn't even get out of bed. He also tries to talk to May in the spirit world. Summer, Ob and May's adopted daughter, tries to be strong for Ob, but finally she cries. She says, "I had tried so hard to bear her loss and had swallowed back the tears that had been building up inside me for two seasons."

In *Letters from Rifka*, Rifka and her family are Russian Jews escaping to America. When they get to Poland, Rifka gets ringworm all over her head and they won't let her on the ship. Her family sails to New York without her and she gets

Continued next page

sent to Belgium by herself to get her disease cured. She says, "Saying good-bye to Mama and Papa hurt in my chest the way it hurt when Saul held me underwater too long." Like Ob, she doesn't even want to go out of her room in Belgium because she misses her parents so much.

In both of these stories, the characters finally survive their pain of missing people by being strong.

ANSWER ORGANIZER

1. Write a topic sentence that names the texts you are comparing and states how they are similar.

    _____

    _____

2. Write two or more sentences about this feature of the first text. If possible, find a quote to prove your point.

    _____

    _____

    _____

    _____

3. Write two or more sentences about this feature of the second text. If possible, find a quote to prove your point.

    _____

    _____

    _____

    _____

4. Write one or two sentences about how this feature was important to both of these texts.

    _____

    _____

    _____

    _____

ANSWER FRAME

The text _____was similar to

_____ because_____

_____.

In the text _____ you can see this

when_____

_____

and also when _____

_____. In the

text _____ you can see this

when_____

_____

and also when_____

_____.

This feature is important to both of these texts because

_____

_____.

QUESTION III.B

What might [character / person] have written in his/ her journal after this happened in the text:_____

_____

PLEASE ANSWER THIS QUESTION FOR THE FOLLOWING TEXT:_____

WHAT YOU NEED TO DO:

1. Before you write: You are pretending to *be* the person or character named in the question. Decide how you would <u>feel</u> about what happened. What would you <u>think</u>?

2. Write a topic sentence that names the event mentioned in the question and tells why it happened.

3. Write a sentence that tells how you feel about this situation.

4. Write one or two details from the text that show *why* you feel this way. (One or two sentences)

5. Write a sentence that tells what you want to happen because of this event.

THE NARRATIVE MODEL
Based on the story *Faithful Elephants* by Yukio Tsuchiya

The question:
What might the elephant trainer have written in his journal after the elephants died?

The answer:

Dear Journal,

My beautiful elephants are dead because of this terrible war. I am so sad about this that I can't stop crying. It was heartbreaking watching them starve to death. They trusted me as their friend. Every time I walked by their cages they just stared at me like they couldn't figure out why I was being so mean, not giving them food. I want all wars to end so there will be no more unnecessary death or suffering for any living creature.

III.B What might [character / person] have written in his/her journal after this
   happened in the text:_____

THE EXPOSITORY MODEL
Based on the article "Young Al" in *Kids Discover:*
Thomas Edison

The question:
What might Thomas Edison have written in his journal on a day
when he had been scolded several times by his teacher for bad
behavior?

The answer:

Dear Journal,

   Today my teacher yelled at me again because I ask too many
questions and keep getting out of my seat. This is making me feel
very discouraged. I don't mean to keep asking questions. It's just
that I'm curious about so many things. Also, I only get out of my
seat because I'd rather experiment with ideas instead of just reading about them in books. I sure hope I'll have a job some day
where it's okay to be curious and experiment with things.

III.B What might [character / person] have written in his/her journal after this happened in the text:_____

ANSWER ORGANIZER

1. Write a topic sentence that names the event mentioned in the question and tells why it happened.

    _____

    _____

2. Write a sentence that tells how you *feel* about this situation.

    _____

    _____

3. Write one detail from the text to show *why* you feel this way.

    _____

    _____

    _____

4. Write a second detail that shows *why* you feel this way.

    _____

    _____

    _____

5. Write a sentence that tells what you want to happen because of this event.

    _____

    _____

III.B What might [character / person] have written in his/her journal after this happened in the text:_____

ANSWER FRAME

Dear Journal,

Something very important just happened: _____

_____.

It happened because_____

_____.

This makes me feel very _____. One

reason I feel this way is _____

_____

_____. Another reason I feel this

way is_____

_____. Because of

this I hope_____

_____.

QUESTION III.C

List _____ questions you would like to ask the author that are not answered in this text. Explain why you would like an answer to each question.

PLEASE ANSWER THIS QUESTION FOR THE FOLLOWING TEXT:_____

WHAT YOU NEED TO DO:

1. Before you write: Reread the text or parts of the text carefully. What did you wonder about as you read? It could be why a character or person acted a certain way, something you disagreed with, something related to the author's word choice, something not answered in the text that you think should have been included, or *any* kind of wondering.

2. Write a sentence that includes your first question.

3. Write one or two sentences explaining why you wonder about this.

4. Write a sentence that includes your second question.

5. Write one or two sentences explaining why you wonder about this.

6. If you are asked to think of more than two questions, repeat steps #4 and #5.

III.C List _____ questions you would like to ask the author that are not answered in this text. Explain why you would like an answer to each question.

THE NARRATIVE MODEL
Based on the fable *"The Bad Kangaroo"* by Arnold Lobel

The question:
Think of two questions you would like to ask Arnold Lobel after reading *"The Bad Kangaroo."* Why would you like answers to these questions?

The answer:

The first question I have for Arnold Lobel is, Why did you choose a kangaroo for the main character in this story? I wonder if kangaroos usually have bad behavior, or maybe the author wanted to use a kangaroo because they are bouncy. My second question for the author is: Why did you have the principal leave before he talked to the small kangaroo's parents? I think he should have stayed and told them that if they stopped doing some of these rude things, maybe their son would stop, too.

III.C List _____ questions you would like to ask the author that are not answered in this text. Explain why you would like an answer to each question.

THE EXPOSITORY MODEL
Based on the story *Welcome to the Green House* by Jane Yolen

The question:
Think of two questions you would like to ask Jane Yolen after reading *Welcome to the Green House.* Why would you like to have answers to these questions?

The answer:

One thing I would like to ask Jane Yolen after finishing this book is: What other animals live in the rainforest? She showed pictures of several animals, but I would just like to know if there are other kinds of wildlife, too. Another question I have for Jane Yolen is: How can kids help to preserve the rainforest? I wish this had been answered in the book because I am a kid who is interested in caring for nature.

III.C List _____ questions you would like to ask the author that are not answered in this text. Explain why you would like an answer to each question.

ANSWER ORGANIZER

1. Write a sentence that contains your first question.

   _____

   _____

2. Write one or two sentences explaining why you wonder about this.

   _____

   _____

   _____

3. Write a sentence that contains your second question.

   _____

   _____

4. Write one or two sentences explaining why you wonder about this.

   _____

   _____

   _____

5. If you need a third question, write it here and also include your reason for asking this question.

   _____

   _____

   _____

III.C List _____ questions you would like to ask the author that are not answered in this text. Explain why you would like an answer to each question.

ANSWER FRAME

One question I would like to ask the author of this text is

_____.

I wonder about this because_____

_____

_____. A second question that

I thought about as I read this is_____

_____.

I would like to know the **answer** to this question because

_____

_____.

A third question not answered in this story is_____

_____.

I am curious about this because_____

_____.

QUESTION III.D

Based on information in this text, what would probably have happened if_____

_____?

PLEASE ANSWER THIS QUESTION FOR THE FOLLOWING TEXT:_____

WHAT YOU NEED TO DO:

1. Write a topic sentence that tells what would have happened *next* in this text if it had been changed the way the question says.

2. Tell one reason *why* this would have happened based on other text events. (One or two sentences)

3. If you can think of a second reason *why* this would have happened, include this reason, too. (One or two sentences)

4. Tell how this change would have affected the outcome of this story or situation.

III.D Based on information in this text, what would probably have happened
if_____?

THE NARRATIVE MODEL
Based on the story *Shiloh* by Phyllis Reynolds Naylor

The question:
Based on information in the story, what would probably have happened if Marty had not found out that Judd Travers shot a deer out-of-season?

The answer:

If Marty hadn't found out that Judd Travers shot a deer out of season, Judd would probably have forced Marty to give Shiloh back to him right then. I think this would have happened because Judd was really mean and he just wanted that dog even though he didn't even like him and kicked him and starved him. He had already made Marty give Shiloh back several times. Also, if Judd hadn't been caught he wouldn't have been afraid Marty would report him and wouldn't have been willing to make a deal with Marty. This would have changed the end of the story from happy to sad because Marty would not have gotten to keep Shiloh for his own.

©2002 Nancy N. Boyles, Teaching Written Response

THE EXPOSITORY MODEL
Based on *Kids Discover: The Civil War*

The question:

Based on the information on pages 6-7, what might have happened if Northern troops had been better prepared at the start of the Civil War?

The answer:

If the Northern troops had been better prepared at the start of the Civil War they probably would have won the first battle which was the Battle of Bull Run. They might have won because they would have been more experienced and they also would have been able to handle guns better. Even though the North did finally win this war, they might have won it much sooner if their soldiers had been better prepared. Fewer people would have lost their lives.

ANSWER ORGANIZER

1. Write a topic sentence that tells what would have happened <u>next</u> in this text if the events had been changed the way the question says.

    _____
    _____

2. Write one or two sentences that tell one reason *why* this would have happened based on other text events.

    _____
    _____
    _____

3. If you can think of **a se**cond reason *why* this would have happened, include this reason, too.

    _____
    _____
    _____

4. Tell how this change would have affected the outcome of this story or situation.

    _____
    _____

III.D **Based on information in this text, what would probably have happened**
   if_____?

ANSWER FRAME

   If the events in this story or situation had been changed the

way the question says, the next thing to happen would probably

be that _____

_____. One

reason this would have happened is because_____

_____. Another reason this might

have happened is because_____

_____.

Even the ending may change. Here is what would probably

happen:_____

_____.

QUESTION III.E

Using information from the text, how do you visualize this scene?

PLEASE ANSWER THIS QUESTION FOR THE FOLLOWING TEXT:_____

WHAT YOU NEED TO DO:

1. Before you write, think of some details that would go along with the feeling or mood the author was trying to create in this text.

2. Write a topic sentence that describes the scene in one or two words (beautiful, scary, messy, peaceful, etc.)

3. Give two or three details *from your imagination* that would add to the mood the author was trying to create. (Two or three sentences)

4. Write a final sentence that tells why these details are important. (What do they show about this situation?)

THE NARRATIVE MODEL
Based on the fable *"The Bad Kangaroo"* by Arnold Lobel

The question:

Using information from the story about the Kangaroo family, what do you think their living room looked like when the principal arrived?

The answer:

I think the Kangaroos' living room was probably a mess. The small kangaroo might have left Legos all over the floor so that people could step on them accidentally and torture their feet. There may have been old newspapers thrown everywhere which would also be a fire hazard. Finally, bags of cookies and candy might be just lying around to get stale and attract ants. All of these things would show even more that the Kangaroo family did not have much common sense.

THE EXPOSITORY MODEL
Based on *Children of Ancient Egypt*, an issue of *Appleseeds*, a Cobblestone Publication

The question:
Using information from the article about "The Boy King" on pages 18-19, try to picture what special things young Pharaoh Tutankhamun might have kept around at his palace?

The answer:

The picture I have of this scene in my head is kind of silly. Beside his velvet robe and a big crown, King Tut might have also had a scooter to ride around the palace grounds if they were popular then, some trading cards for when he played with other kids (if they were invented 3,300 years ago), and maybe even a beach ball for playing in the Nile River. King Tut might have had these things because he became the pharaoh of Egypt when he was only nine years old. He was just a kid and I think he would have wanted some toys even though he was a powerful ruler.

ANSWER ORGANIZER

1. Write a topic sentence that describes the scene in one or two words (beautiful, scary, messy, peaceful, etc.)

    _____

    _____

2. Give one detail *from your imagination* that would add to the mood the author was trying to create.

    _____

    _____

3. Give a second detail *from your imagination* that would add to the mood the author was trying to create.

    _____

    _____

4. Give a third detail *from your imagination* that would add to the mood the author was trying to create.

    _____

    _____

5. Write a final sentence that tells why these details would fit into this scene.

    _____

    _____

ANSWER FRAME

One word or phrase I would use to describe this scene in the text is _____. Here are some details the author might have added to paint an even clearer picture of this in the reader's mind. One detail might be that

_____

_____.

Another detail might be that_____

_____.

A third detail might be that_____

_____.

These details would all fit into this scene because_____

_____.

QUESTION III.F

Does [something or someone] in this text remind you of [something or someone] in your own life? Explain or describe.

PLEASE ANSWER THIS QUESTION FOR THE FOLLOWING TEXT:_____

WHAT YOU NEED TO DO:

1. Write a topic sentence that tells *who* or *what* in the text is similar to something in your own life.

2. Give at least two examples of how this character, person, or situation is the same.

3. Try to think of one way that this character, person, or situation is *different* from something in your life.

4. Write a final sentence that explains what these similarities or differences show about the character, person, or situation.

©2002 Nancy N. Boyles, Teaching Written Response

III.F **Does [something or someone] in this text remind you of [something or someone] in your own life? Explain or describe.**

THE NARRATIVE MODEL
Based on *Frindle* by Andrew Clements

The question:
How does Mrs. Granger, Nick's teacher, remind you of a teacher in your own life?

The answer:

In some ways Mrs. Granger, Nick's fifth grade teacher, reminded me of a teacher that I had one time. Her name was Miss Markley and she loved the dictionary, too. Every week we had to look up all 20 of our spelling words and write the definitions. We also had to write the pronunciation for each word (BORING). But the worst thing was that if you were bad, you had to copy a whole dictionary page for punishment. I don't think Mrs. Granger would make her students do that. She seemed to care about words. Sometimes I think Mrs. Markley just cared about keeping us busy and quiet.

THE EXPOSITORY MODEL

Based on "Thomas Edison," an issue of *Kids Discover Magazine.*

The question:

Does "Young Al" remind you of anyone you know? How are they alike? Are they different in any way? Use information from pages 6 and 7 to support your answer.

The answer:

Young Al reminds me a lot of my cousin Roy. Al was very curious and so is my cousin. Both of them have done some pretty weird things because of their curiosity. For example, once Al sat on some goose eggs hoping they would hatch. He also burned down a barn because he wanted to find out about fire. Roy didn't do anything that dangerous. But he did cut his sister's hair to find out how it would look short. Another time he ordered something from the Internet without his parents' permission just because it sounded good. Al and Roy are different though because Al always got in trouble in school. I don't think that happens to Roy.

III.F Does [something or someone] in this text remind you of [something or someone] in your own life? Describe or explain.

ANSWER ORGANIZER

1. Write a topic sentence that tells *who* or *what* in the story is similar to something in your own life.

   _____

   _____

2. Give at least two examples of how this character or situation is the *same*.

   _____

   _____

   _____

   _____

3. Try to think of one way that this character or situation is *different* from something in your life.

   _____

   _____

4. Write a final sentence that explains what these similarities or differences show about the character or situation.

   _____

   _____

III.F Does [something or someone] in this text remind you of [something or someone] in your own life? Explain or describe.

ANSWER FRAME

In this story, _____ is similar

to_____ in my own life. For

example, _____

_____

_____.

Another similarity is that _____

_____

_____.

One *difference* that I noticed is that _____

_____

_____. I think

that these similarities and differences show that _____

_____

_____.

QUESTION III.G

If you had been [person / character], how would you have handled the situation when_____

_____?

PLEASE ANSWER THIS QUESTION FOR THE FOLLOWING TEXT:_____

WHAT YOU NEED TO DO:

1. Write a sentence that explains a little about what led up to this situation and tells how the person handled it. (Maybe you can even find a quote to support what you say.)

2. Write a sentence that tells whether you would have handled the situation the *same* way or *differently*.

3. If you would handle the situation the same way, write a sentence explaining *why*.

    If you would handle the situation differently, write one or two sentences explaining *why not*, and tell what you would do instead.

THE NARRATIVE MODEL
Based on the story *Mississippi Bridge* by Mildred D. Taylor

The question:
If you had been Josias, how would you have handled the situation when Pa accused him of lying about being offered a "cash paying job" from his cousin?

The answer:

When Pa accused Josias of lying about having a real job, Josias got scared and backed down. He said he hadn't told the truth and that he really didn't have a job. If I had been Josias, a black man in the South in the 1930s, I probably would have done the same thing. Back then it seems like white people had all the power and black people had none.   I would have been scared Pa would torture me if I didn't say what he wanted.

THE EXPOSITORY MODEL
Based on the chapter "At Work" in *Immigrant Kids* by Russell Freedman

The question:
If you had been Leonard Covelo's parents, how would you have handled the situation when Leonard told you he had gotten a job?

The answer:

When Leonard told his parents he had found a job delivering bakery goods early in the morning before school, they were really proud of him. His father said, "Good. You are becoming a man now."   If I had been Leonard's parents, I don't think I would have said that. Leonard was only twelve years old. If he was my child I would say, "Stay in bed until it's time for school because I want you to be able to do your best work."

III.G If you had been [person / character], how would you have handled the situation when_____?

ANSWER ORGANIZER

1. Write a sentence that explains a little about what led up to this situation and tells how the person handled it.

   _____
   _____
   _____

2. Write a sentence that tells whether you would have handled the situation the *same* way or *differently*.

   _____
   _____

3. If you would handle the situation the same way, write a sentence explaining *why*.

   OR

   If you would handle the situation differently, write one or two sentences explaining *why not*, and tell what you would do instead.

   _____
   _____
   _____
   _____

III.G If you had been [person / character], how would you have handled the situation when_____?

ANSWER FRAME

Here is how _____ handled the

situation when _____

_____.

This is what s/he did: _____

_____

_____. If I had been

_____ I would have handled this problem

the same way/ a different way because _____

_____

_____. Here is what I

would have done:_____

_____.

QUESTION III.H

How is [someone or something described in this text] similar to someone or something in our world today?

PLEASE ANSWER THIS QUESTION FOR THE FOLLOWING TEXT:_____

WHAT YOU NEED TO DO:

1. Write a topic sentence that tells who or what it is from real life that you are comparing to something from the text.

2. Write a sentences explaining how these are similar.

3. Give at least two examples that show this similarity. (You might want to use a quote for extra support.)

4. Try to think of one way these people, situations, or things are different and write a sentence about this difference.

III.H   How is [someone or something described in this text] similar to someone or something in our world today?

THE NARRATIVE MODEL
Based on *Pink and Say* by Patricia Polacco

The question:
Compare Moe Moe Bay to someone in your own life.

The answer:

Moe Moe Bay is a lot like my grandmother. These two women are very similar because they are both very, very kind.

In the story, Moe Moe comforts Say when he tells her he is a coward. She answers, "You ain't nothin' of the kind. You a child...a child!" My grandmother comforts me, sometimes too, like when I got a bad grade on my math test, and she said it was okay because I tried my hardest. Moe Moe also thinks of other people before herself. She even got killed to protect Pink and Say. My grandmother didn't have to do anything that brave, but she always asks me what I want for dinner when we go to her house, and she cooks me my favorite meals. One way that Moe Moe and my grandma are *not* the same is that Moe Moe was living during a terrible war. My grandma lives in a peaceful time and her life isn't in danger.

THE EXPOSITORY MODEL
Based on *Knights in Shining Armor* by Gail Gibbons

The question:
Compare the *knights* in this book to someone or something in our world today.

The answer:

I think that the knights of long ago were a lot like the war generals we have today. They were both in charge of protecting people in a time of war. For both, you have to move up through the ranks, like page and squire before you become a knight, and private and corporal and other titles before you become a general. Also, they fought over the same kinds of things, such as land and property. One difference is that knights wore armor while generals wear camouflage clothing to keep them safe.

ANSWER ORGANIZER

1.   Write a topic sentence that tells the two people or things you are comparing (one from the text and the other from real life).

   _____

   _____

2.   Write a sentence that tells how these are similar.

   _____

   _____

3.   Give one example of this similarity. (You can add a quote for extra support.)

   _____

   _____

4.   Give another example of this similarity. (You can add a quote for extra support.)

   _____

   _____

5.   Give one example of how these two people or things are *different*.

   _____

   _____

III.H How is [someone or something] in this text similar to someone or something in our world today?

ANSWER FRAME

_____ from the text is a lot like

_____in our world today. These are

similar because_____

_____

_____.

Another way these are *similar* is _____

_____

_____.

One way these are *different* is _____

_____

_____.

QUESTION III.I

What do you think will happen next? Use information from the text to support your answer.

PLEASE ANSWER THIS QUESTION FOR THE FOLLOWING TEXT:_____

WHAT YOU NEED TO DO:

1. Write one or two sentences that explain how this story / article / chapter ends.

2. Write one or two sentences that tell what you think will happen next.

3. By looking back at the text, decide *why* this is likely to happen. (Use a quote from the text to provide extra support for your point of view if possible.) You will need about two sentences for your proof.

4. Write one final sentence telling why you think it's good or not so good that this will probably happen.

THE NARRATIVE MODEL
Based on the story, *Missing May* by Cynthia Rylant

The question:

What do you think would happen next if this story continued beyond the final chapter that Cynthia Rylant wrote? Use information from the text to support your answer.

The answer:

In the last chapter of this story Summer finally cries about May's death and then she feels much better. She, Ob, and Cletus go out into May's old garden and fill it up with Ob's whirligigs so that they may finally have a place to fly and live.   If there was another chapter in this book I think it would show that Summer is now happier. The story says, "There was a tranquillity in me that felt all right." Maybe she would plant some flowers in May's garden and have a big party there with the beautiful flowers and whirligigs as decorations. I think it would be good if this really happened because then I would know for sure that Summer was not sad any more.

III.I   What do you think will happen next? Use information from the text to support your answer.

THE EXPOSITORY MODEL
Based on the chapter "At Work" in *Immigrant Kids*

The question:
What do you think would happen next if this chapter continued and told about how working conditions changed for the immigrants? Use information from the text to support your answer.

The answer:

    This chapter talks about how hard it was for immigrants to make a living when they arrived in America. Even the children had to help out because their families needed the money so much. The chapter says, "Kids eight or ten years old worked in factories, warehouses, laundries, and stores. Almost everyone over fourteen was employed full time." If this chapter continued, it might tell about how the laws were changed so young children could not go to work while they were so young because that really did happen eventually. I think it would be good if the book included this information because I would like to know when these laws got changed.

What do you think will happen next? Use information from the text to support your answer.

ANSWER ORGANIZER

1. Write one or two sentences to explain how this story / chapter / article ends.

    _____

    _____

    _____

2. Write one or two sentences that tell *what* you think will happen next.

    _____

    _____

    _____

3. Write one or two sentences to explain *why* you think this will happen next. (Use a quote for extra support.)

    _____

    _____

    _____

4. Write a sentence that tells why you think it's good, or not so good that this could happen next.

    _____

    _____

III.I **What do you think will happen next? Use information from the text to support your answer.**

ANSWER FRAME

Here is what is happening in this part of the reading:_____

_____

_____.

The thing that could happen next might be_____

_____

_____.

I think this might happen because _____

_____

_____.

Here is a quote from the reading to prove my point:_____

_____

_____.

I think it would be good / not good if this happened because

_____

_____.

QUESTION III.J

Imagine that you are giving a talk to your class about _____. Using information from the text, write two ideas that you would use in this speech.

PLEASE ANSWER THIS QUESTION FOR THE FOLLOWING TEXT: _____

WHAT YOU NEED TO DO:

1. Write a sentence that names one important idea about this topic.

2. Write a detail about this idea.

3. Write a sentence that names a second important idea about this topic.

4. Write a detail about your second idea.

©2002 Nancy N. Boyles, Teaching Written Response

III.1 Imagine that you are giving a talk to your class about _____.
Using information from the text, write two ideas that you would use in this speech.

THE NARRATIVE MODEL
Based on the story "Lightning Rod" by Dan Gutman in *Storyworks***, February/March 1997**

The question:
Imagine that you are giving a talk to your class about <u>psychokinesis</u>. Using information from the text, write two ideas you would use in your speech.

The answer:

One idea I would explain in a speech about psychokinesis is that this term means you can move objects just by using your mind. In this story Rod figures out he has psychokinesis when he can get the car window to roll up without touching the handle.

A second important idea about psychokinesis is that some people get this power after receiving a strong electric shock. Rod got this strange power when he was struck by a bolt of lighthning.

THE EXPOSITORY MODEL
Based on the chapter "At Play" from *Immigrant Kids* by Russell Freedman

The question:

Imagine that you are giving a talk to your class about immigrant kids at school. Using information from the text, write two ideas you would use in your speech.

The answer:

One important idea I would explain in a speech about immigrant kids at school is that they had to be in classes with younger children until they learned English. This made them feel really humiliated and they didn't like this system.

Another important idea is that these schools didn't have any luxuries. There were no playgrounds or gyms and the toilets were in the yard. Instead of playing sports, students just stood at their desks doing fitness exercises.

III.I   **Imagine that you are giving a talk to your class about _____.**
Using information from the text, write two ideas that you would use in this speech.

ANSWER ORGANIZER

1. Write a sentence that names one important idea about this
    topic that you would include in a speech.

    _____

    _____

2. Write one detail about this idea from the text.

    _____

    _____

    _____

3. Write a sentence that includes a second idea about this topic
    that you would include in a speech.

    _____

    _____

4. Write one detail about this idea from the text.

    _____

    _____

    _____

III.I Imagine that you are giving a talk to your class about _____.
Using information from the text, write two ideas that you would use in this speech.

ANSWER FRAME

One important idea I would explain in a talk to my class about

_____ is

_____.

A detail about this from the text about this is _____

_____

_____.

Another important idea I would explain in a talk about this topic is

_____

_____.

A detail about this from the text is _____

_____

_____.

PART THREE

Additional Resources

Texts Used for Modeled Responses

With as many children's books as my library contains, you might think that selecting the literature to use as models would be a "non-issue." (Just grab the first few volumes that fall off the shelf.) Of course that would be much too simple. Initially, I was looking for one "perfect" narrative and another "perfect" expository source. It quickly became apparent that this was a bad idea because there is no "perfect book" out there that invites contemplation in all of these realms of thinking. And even if such a book could be found, I wouldn't want to center every question around a single selection. I do not want to send the message that it would ever be desirable to ask so many questions about any one piece of text. A more prudent approach is to connect reading and written response judiciously, intentionally, and thoroughly.

As I pondered book possibilities I looked for favorite authors, a variety of genres, quality works that were mostly short, and/or works with which many middle-grade students would already be familiar. It is *not* essential that children have prior knowledge of text selections used for answer models. However, this might make the instruction more fun.

Furthermore, the texts I include here have been tested in many classrooms and are great additions to the literary knowledge-base of all readers. The fact that most of these are quick reads makes them extra-easy to share in a classroom read-aloud. That they are mostly available in paperback may be an added incentive. **IMPORTANT:** A brief **annotation** follows each narrative and expository selection, along with the approximate **reading level (RL)** and **interest level (IL)** — both expressed as grade levels. For example, "RL 4" means that the approximate reading level is fourth grade. "IL 3-7" means the interest level is third grade through seventh grade.

Narrative Selections

Frindle by Andrew Clements (RL 4, IL 3-7)

This humorous tale about a fifth grader who invents a new word for "pen" — to the obvious displeasure of his classroom teacher — ultimately causes kids and teachers alike to celebrate the power of ingenuity and the creative spirit.

Lily's Crossing by Patricia Reilly Giff (RL 4, IL 4-7)

Set during World War II, this story centers around 10-year-old Lily, and her interactions with family and special friends. Giff succeeds in depicting Lily quite realistically, imperfections and all. One of Lily's less endearing habits is lying, which ultimately causes a very close call for a young Hungarian boy who has recently immigrated to the United States.

Letters from Rifka by Karen Hesse (RL 4, IL 4-8)

If you're looking for a "strong girl" story, this is a great choice. Rifka, a Russian Jew during World War I, flees her native land along with her family, in search of a better life in America. Intelligence, cleverness, and perseverance provide the keys to surmounting obstacles that appear for Rifka at nearly every turn in the road.

"The Bad Kangaroo" in *Fables* by Arnold Lobel (RL 4, IL 2-6)

The Bad Kangaroo is one of 20 tales in this delightful book of fables with an updated twist and lively illustrations. Although the tales are all wonderful for developing students' inferential thinking, this fable is my true favorite. Children like it; teachers love it. Read it and smile.

Shiloh by Phyllis Reynolds Nailor (RL 4, IL 3-7)

What is it about dog stories that provide such universal appeal to students of all ages? There are many fine dogs roaming around children's literature for us to admire (Old Yeller, Lassie, and Balto among others). But somehow, Shiloh seems to nudge out the rest for a special place close to readers' hearts.

Pink and Say by Patricia Polacco (RL 5, IL 4-7)

I could have selected any work by Patricia Polacco, author of numerous picture books, for each is wonderful in its own way. While children of any age would enjoy these stories, I feel that older readers can best appreciate the more subtle features of this author's meaningful messages. This particular story revolves around two young boys during the Civil War, one black and one white, who become friends by circumstance, and who together face the horrors of war in a highly personal way.

Missing May by Cynthia Rylant (RL 5, IL 5-8)

Also high on my list of favorite authors is Cynthia Rylant, whose characters and plots always seem to jump up off the page and move right into my life. So it is with *Missing May*, in which Rylant brings together three unlikely individuals, all of whom discover more about themselves as they cope with May's death. Here it's not just the story, but the *telling* of the story (all those fabulous craft elements) that make this thin volume such a powerful read.

Mississippi Bridge by Mildred D. Taylor (RL 4, IL 3-6)

This story isn't as well-known as *Roll of Thunder, Hear My Cry*, which is probably Taylor's best known work. But it's a great choice for middle-graders because it's short, it brings back the same characters students have met in Taylor's other works, and it packs a *big* punch. The 1930s-Mississippi setting is the scene of horrific racial discrimination — with some ironic results. It's a kid's-eye view of the American South before Civil Rights.

Faithful Elephants by Yukio Tsuchiya (RL 5, IL 5-8)

This is a not-for-little-kids picture book. It seems that during World War II, the people of Japan realized that the atomic bomb would be dropped on their country. Authorities made the difficult decision to systematically kill all the animals in Japan's zoos because they worried that a bomb might allow them to break free and run wild in the streets. What follows is the heart- wrenching saga of two zookeepers as they carry out this command, killing three beautiful elephants. Yes, the story is an important one as it shares a perspective of this war that we seldom consider. But no, even the muted watercolor illustrations do not soften the intensity of this tragic and true narrative.

Expository Selections

Children of Ancient Egypt (RL 4, IL 3-6) an issue of *Appleseeds*, a **Cobblestone Publication**

> *Appleseeds* is written at an early-intermediate reading level, which sets it apart from other Cobblestone publications that are more appropriate for late elementary or middle-school levels. Like other Cobblestone resources, this one is a monthly, theme-based magazine. It contains both narrative and expository articles and hands-on activities also related to the theme. Graphics are attractive without being overwhelming.

Dinner at Aunt Connie's House **by Faith Ringgold (RL 5, IL 2-6)**

> This picture book presents expository information wrapped inside a narrative. Young Melody and her brother Lonnie explore the attic after dining at Aunt Connie's house, only to discover twelve beautiful paintings of famous African-American women. The paintings then come alive and talk to the children, with each woman describing her role in American history. Although the information presented is quite basic, the format of this book is interesting from the perspective of writer's craft. And the illustrations certainly demonstrate (in the words of the author) "that art can be more than a picture on a wall — it can envision our history and illustrate proud events in people's lives."

Welcome to the Green House **by Jane Yolen, illustrated by Laura Regan (RL 3, IL 2-5)**

> This text offers another wonderful opportunity to show children that picture books are not necessarily narrative. Furthermore, its rhythmic exploration of the sounds and colors of flora and fauna in the rainforest is testimony to the fact that expository writing need not be dull and lifeless. The vibrant illustrations further dramatize the pictures painted with words.

Welcome to the Sea of Sand **by Jane Yolen, illustrated by Laura Regan (RL 3, IL 2-5)**

> Same author and illustrator, same technique, different subject. Welcome to Arizona's Sonora Desert. It's another poetic tribute to the power of kid-friendly expository writing.

We Came to North America: The Africans **by Jen Green (RL 7, IL 4-8)**

> This is part of a paperback series published by Crabtree which highlights different immigrant groups that have arrived in North America and

contributed something special. Very readable at the upper-intermediate level, it is clearly written and simply laid out. Other groups featured in the series are Chinese, French, Hispanics, Italians, and Jews.

"Thomas Edison" and "The Civil War," issues of *Kids Discover Magazine* (RL 6, IL 4-8)

These monthly theme-based periodicals cover a huge range of topics annually, spanning many content areas, with the reading level most appropriate for upper-elementary and middle-school students. Text is supported with high-quality graphics. However, multiple columns and several subcategories often addressed on a single page make the format confusing for some students. Still, these thin volumes are packed with great information and make wonderful supplementary resources for social studies and science.

Immigrant Kids by Russell Freedman (RL 5, IL 4-8)

Scholastic publishes a variety of soft-cover resources targeted to specific topics. This one, about the lives of children who came to America in the late 1800s and early 1900s, provides written and visual snapshots of what it was like to be young and a newly arrived citizen in this country during that time in our history. Interspersed are first-person accounts and many black-and-white photos that capture the true spirit of this experience.

Oh, Freedom: Kids Talk about the Civil Rights Movement with the People who Made it Happen by Casey King and Linda Barrett Osborne (RL 6, IL 4-8)

Another Scholastic publication similar to the one described above. This one is primarily a compilation of interviews: children discussing the Civil Rights movement with the people who made it happen — a few famous names and many more unsung heroes. These first-person accounts and accompanying photos really help middle-grade readers connect with these voices from the past. The oral history/interview format offers students another alternative model, as well, for the presentation of their own expository writing.

The Day Martin Luther King, Jr. was Shot: A Photo History of the Civil Rights Movement by Jim Haskins (RL 6, IL 5-8)

Yet one more resource from Scholastic. This text begins on April 4, 1968, the day Martin Luther King, Jr., was shot and then flashes back to the slave trade and a chronicle of significant moments in the quest for racial equality. Graphics are black-and-white, mostly photographs, and powerful. This book would best match the interests and reading levels of middle-schoolers.

The Heart **by Seymour Simon (RL 4, IL 3-7)**

You can't talk about well-written expository text for children without mentioning Seymour Simon. This is but one of his books with a science theme and combines readable information for intermediate-grade students in a large font with full-page, colorful illustrations to support the text. (Science books were never like this when I was in elementary school!)

Knights in Shining Armor **by Gail Gibbons (RL 4, IL 2-5)**

With more than 80 informational books to her credit, expository resources by Gail Gibbons abound. The picture-book format, cartoon-like illustrations, and easy-to-read text make her work appealing to intermediate-grade students reading below level, and also to primary-grade kids.

The Tree That Would Not Die **by Ellen Levine (RL 3, IL 2-5)**

While purists may object to the inclusion of this title in the expository category (after all, it does tell a story), I believe I can defend its placement: In this picture book, 400 years of American history come alive through the "eyes" of a tree that was poisoned in 1989. While this tale entertains, to an even greater degree, it informs. We see here, too, another rich possibility for students' own expository writing: an inanimate object's "first person" perspective.

Details about Details

I have often thought that if students could *identify* details in literature, they would be more successful at incorporating them into their own writing. I consulted resources by some of my favorite "writing people" — Marcia Freeman, Barry Lane, Ralph Fletcher, and Katie Wood Ray. I translated their suggestions for understanding and using details into terms that made the most sense to me, and added a few of my own in order to compile the following list. Here are different kinds of details that kids can look for in order to support their general claims about text:

Physical description of someplace, someone, or something

"There is no roof in the green house,
only the canopy of leaves,
where the sun and rain
poke through narrow slots;" (n.p.)
Welcome to the Sea of Sand, by Jane Yolen

"There was once a velveteen rabbit, and in the beginning he was really splendid. He was fat and bunchy, as a rabbit should be; his coat was spotted brown and white, he had real thread whiskers, and his ears were lined with pink sateen." (13)
The Velveteen Rabbit, by Margery Williams

"The bathroom floor was covered with gray water. Water was struggling down the drain with a sucking chug. The tub was black with dirt, a greasy darker ring encircling the inside like a filthy belt." (47)
Randall's Wall, by Carol Fenner

A private thought

"I stood there a while trying to remember how to begin my windup.
Which do I lift first. . . my left leg or my right leg? And then what? Is there a hop involved? Or a skip? Or a jump?" (45)
Skinny-Bones, by Barbara Park

Gesture

"I heard something like whistling. I looked up. It *was* whistling. It was coming from a funny-looking dorky little runt walking up the sidewalk. Only he wasn't just walking regular. He was walking like he owned the place, both hands in his pockets, sort of swaying lah-dee-dah with each step. Strolllll-ing. Strolling and gawking at the houses and whistling a happy little dorky tune like some Sneezy or Snoozy or whatever their names are." (2)
Crash, by Jerry Spinelli

Show (Don't tell)

"Ann Marie relaxed the clenched fingers of her right hand, which still clutched Ellen's necklace. She looked down, and saw that she had imprinted the Star of David into her palm." (49)
Number the Stars, by Lois Lowry

Dialogue

"That new dog of yours run off again?" Dad asks him.

"I swear to God I find him this time, I'm goin' to break his legs," Judd says, and spits.

"Oh, come on, Judd. A dog with four broke legs ain't no dog to you at all." (52)

Shiloh, by Phyllis Reynolds Naylor

Interesting comparison

"My papa's hair is like a broom,
all up in the air."

Hairs/Pelitos, by Sandra Cisneros (n.p.)

"My teacher is Miss Bonkers,
She's as bouncy as a flea." (n.p.)

Hooray for Diffendoofer Day!, by Dr. Seuss with some help from Jack Prelutsky and Lane Smith

Proper nouns

"....I saw Oreos and Ruffles and big bags of Snickers....I saw fat bags of marsh-mallows and cans of SpaghettiOs and a little plastic bear full of honey." (8)

Missing May, by Cynthia Rylant

Examples

"Milo kept imagining what it would be like to be a perfect person. He'd be able to do anything he wanted to and do it right the first time. He would be able to throw out all his erasers. He could correct his teachers in front of the class and never be wrong. He'd get perfect scores on all his tests." *(17)*

Be a Perfect Person in Just Three Days, by Stephen Manes

Anecdotes

"At home most of Eleanor's waking hours were spent alone with her nanny, who spoke to Eleanor only in French. When she and Nanny went to the park, the nannies would gather together to gossip. But while the other children played happily, Eleanor clung close to Nanny's skirts." (n.p.)

Eleanor, by Barbara Cooney

Definitions

"Soap was made from a mixture of **tallow**, or melted animal fat, and a strong, burning chemical called **lye**. (9)

Women of the West, by Bobbie Kalman

Facts

"There were two kinds of slave sales: public auctions and scrambles."

We Came to North America: The Africans, by Jen Green

Books to Teach Comprehension Strategies

Keene, E. & Zimmermann, S. (1997). *Mosaic of thought: Teaching comprehension in a reader's workshop*. Portsmouth, NH: Heinemann.

Everyone is talking about this book! It identifies (based on research) seven comprehension strategies that separate good readers from struggling readers. The authors provide classroom scenarios through which we can visualize the kind of instruction that leads to an understanding of these key strategies in a reading workshop format. Instructional prompts to elicit students' strategic thinking make this a highly practical resource.

Harvey, S. & Goudvis, A. (2000). *Strategies that work: Teaching comprehension to enhance understanding*. York, ME: Stenhouse.

This is a very classroom-friendly book. It contains more than 40 K-8 strategy lessons divided among the seven comprehension strategies. It addresses both fiction and nonfiction and also includes extensive bibliographies of short texts useful for strategy application.

Allen, J. (2000). *Yellow brick roads: Shared and guided paths to independent reading 4-12*. York, ME: Stenhouse.

This book is especially well-matched to the needs of middle-school teachers, providing strategy lessons, extensive bibliographies (including bibliographies of web sites), insights into issues related to struggling readers at the middle-school level, and many graphic organizers.

Tovini, C. (2000). *I read it, but I don't get it: Comprehension strategies for adolescent reades* York, ME: Stenhouse.

This is another book of techniques for teaching the essential comprehension strategies and contains many of the same features as the book above. This author, who is a teacher of adolescents, has a great sense of humor. Easy to read.

Wilhelm, J. (2001). *Strategic reading: Guiding students to lifelong literacy 6-12*. Portsmouth, NH: Heinemann.

The thing I like best about this book is that it correlates strategy learning with explicit instruction. Wilhelm discusses the mismatch that commonly exists at the middle/secondary level between teachers' expectations and students' literacy skills. Dozens of innovative strategies are offered that empower students both as readers *and* as lifelong learners.

Boyles, N. (2004). *Constructing meaning through kid-friendly comprehension strategy instruction*. Gainesville, FL: Maupin House.

This resource shows you how to teach the reader *and* the reading by applying the explicit teaching model to comprehension strategy instruction.

Resources Related to Explicit Instruction

Hancock, J. (ed.) (1999). *The explicit teaching of reading.* **Newark, DE: International Reading Association.**

This is a wonderful resource for teachers who want to learn more about *what* explicit instruction is all about, and *why* it is such a wonderful instructional model, especially within the framework of literacy education. Different authors discuss the application of explicit instruction to topics such as literature circles, metacognition, and nonfiction texts. A very readable little book.

Hunter, M. (1995). *Mastery teaching.* **Thousand Oaks, CA: Corwin Press.**

This classic in the field of explicit teaching has been around for many years (recently reprinted in paperback) and is credited with changing the instructional practices of thousands of teachers and perhaps, the learning outcomes of hundreds of thousands of students. The premise of this text is that "mastery teaching produces mastery learning." Explicit instruction, claims Hunter, increases motivation, can make material meaningful, helps students to remember, and provides for transfer.

Jones, F. (1987). *Positive classroom instruction.* **New York: McGraw-Hill Book Company.**

Great book! Fred Jones considers his model of explicit instruction "the basic building block of the entire educational enterprise — a single lesson well taught." A highlight of this text is the author's treatment of a "huge blind spot" in the delivery of most lessons: That topic is the means by which teachers give corrective feedback to students. Teachers will learn a lot of very practical things from this book — and will also enjoy Jones' entertaining, witty style.

Swartz, R. & Parks, S. (1994). *Infusing the teaching of critical and creative thinking into content instruction.* **Pacific Grove, CA: Critical Thinking Press & Software.**

This hefty teachers' resource book turns content lessons into direct, explicit instruction with a focus on critical and creative thinking. It contains sample lessons at different grade levels and many graphic organizers to help teachers create their own lessons. Some of the skills included are decision making, problem-solving, comparing and contrasting, sequencing, and predicting.

Name_____ **Date**_____

PROVE IT!...

1. Read page _____ and find a sentence that proves that

    _____

    Proof: _____

    _____

    _____

2. Read page _____ and find a sentence that proves that

    _____

    Proof: _____

    _____

    _____

Teaching Written Response to Text and Best Practice

Teaching Written Response to Text works. It works because it integrates about a million (plus or minus a few thousand) elements of **Best Practice**. (Here are just a few.)

Consistent with Constructivist Learning Theory
Effective lessons must include opportunities for experimenting, examining models, reflecting, recognizing patterns, and creating personal responses.

Brooks and Brooks, 1993

Incorporates Scaffolded Instruction
In teaching the student, the metaphor of a scaffold is used to describe supports that the teacher provides for the student in the early stages of learning a task that is beyond the student's level of competency. These supports are removed when they are no longer necessary.

Stone, 1998; Rosenshine, 1997

Promotes Reading Engagement
Learners become engaged in literacy in part as they grow more strategic.

Alvermann and Guthrie, 1994

Focuses on Essential Strategies
There are very few, but very essential thinking processes associated with proficient reading that are common to proficient readers of many ages. These processes or cognitive strategies can be taught systematically.

Keene and Zimmermann, 1997

Focuses on Explicit Teaching
Explicit teaching is about making the hidden obvious; exposing and explaining what is taken for granted; demystifying mental processes; letting children in on the information and strategies which will enable them to become powerful literacy users.

Wilkinson, 1995

Focuses on Effective Questioning
There are many different kinds of questions, but the recommendation is that you avoid relying too heavily on closed, convergent questions. Experts also recommend that when teachers ask personal-opinion questions, they should require that students explain, elaborate, and support their responses. As much as possible, they should be asked to define their criteria for judging.

Kingen, 2000

Honors Different Learning Modalities
Some students learn best with their ears, picking up ideas more completely when they get or work with them auditorily. In contrast, some students prefer the visual mode; they are at their best when they receive input through their eyes and express it visually. For other students, touch is especially important in their thinking and learning.

Hennings, 1997

Supports and Extends the Reading Process for All Students, Including Readers with Learning Disabilities
Students with learning disabilities need explicit structured instruction to learn reading comprehension skills. Incidental, literature-based instruction that is typically used to teach reading comprehension is not sufficient.

Williams, 1998

Connects Reading and Writing

Reading and writing are each enhanced when they are taught and learned together and when learners draw upon information from both processes.

Shanahan and Lomax, 1986

Supports Writing in the Content Areas

Writing in the content areas is useful because it helps students to reflect on, elaborate on, and extend ideas and experiences. Writing causes the writer to think through relations among ideas.

Langer and Applebee, 1987

Promotes Analytic Assessment

Although a holistic score can be useful to provide a snapshot of writing achievement, its flaw is that it provides little information that can be used to plan and develop subsequent instruction. Analytic assessment, by comparison, provides the most information from which to draw conclusions about writers and writing. Specific elements of the writing are examined individually.

Dahl and Farnan, 1998

References

Alvermann, D.E., & Guthrie, J.T. (1994). The director's corner. *NRRC News: A Newsletter of the National Reading Research Center*. Athens, GA: National Reading Research Center.

Beaver, T. (1998). *The author's profile: Assessing writing in context*. York, ME: Stenhouse.

Brooks, J.G., & Brooks, M.G. (1993). *In search of understanding: The case for constructivist classrooms*. Alexandria, VA: Association for Supervision and Curriculum Development.

Cisneros, S. (1994). *Hairs/Pelitos*. New York: Alfred A. Knopf.

Clements, A. (1996). *Frindle*. New York: Simon & Schuster.

Cooney, B. (1999). *Eleanor*. New York: Scholastic.

Dahl, K.L., & Farnan, N. (1998). *Children's writing: Perspectives from research*. Newark, DE: International Reading Association.

Fletcher, R. (1993). *What a writer needs*. Portsmouth, NH: Heinemann.

Fletcher, R & Portalupi, J. (1998). *Craft lessons: Teaching writing K-8*. York, ME: Stenhouse.

Freedman, R. (1980). *Immigrant kids*. New York: Scholastic.

Freeman, M. (1997). *Listen to this: Developing an ear for expository*. Gainesville, FL: Maupin House.

_____ (1998). *Teaching the youngest writers: A practical guide*. Gainesville, FL: Maupin House.

Garner, E. R. (1999). *Eleanor's story: An American girl in Hitler's Germany*. Atlanta, GA: Peachtree Publishers.

Gibbons, G. (1995). *Knights in shining armor*. New York: Little, Brown and Company.

Giff, P.. (1997). *Lily's crossing*. New York: Bantam Doubleday Dell.

Green, J. (2000). *We came to North America: The Africans*. New York: Crabtree Publishing.

Hancock, J. (ed.) (1999). *The explicit teaching of reading*. Newark, DE: International Reading Association.

Haskins, J. (1992). *The day Martin Luther King, Jr. was shot: A photo history of the Civil Rights Movement*. New York: Scholastic.

Hennings, D.G. (1997). Diversity in the multicultural classroom. In *Communication in action: Teaching literature-based language arts*. Boston: Houghton Mifflin.

Hesse, K. (1992). *Letters from Rifka*. New York: Puffin Books.

Hunter, M. (1995). *Mastery teaching*. Thousand Oaks, CA: Corwin Press.

Jones, F. (1987). *Positive classroom instruction*. New York: McGraw- Hill Book Company.

Kalman, B (2000). *Women of the west*. New York: Crabtree Publishing.

Keene, E. & Zimmerman, S. (1997). *Mosaic of thought*. Portsmouth, NH: Heinemann.

King, C. & Osborne, B. (1997). *Oh, freedom: Kids talk about the Civil Rights movement with the people who made it happen*. New York: Scholastic.

Kingen, S. (2000). *Teaching language arts in middle schools*. Mahwah, NJ: Lawrence Erlbaum Associates.

Lane, B. (1993). *After the end: Teaching and learning creative revision*. Portsmouth, NH: Heinemann.

Langer, J.A., & Applebee, A.N. (1987). *How writing shapes thinking*. Urbana, IL: National Council of Teachers of English.

Levine, E. (1995). *The tree that would not die*. New York: Scholastic.

Lobel. A. (1980). *Fables*. New York: Harper and Row.

Lowry, L. (1989). *Number the stars*. New York: Dell Publishing.

Manes, S. (1982). *Be a perfect person in just three days*. New York: Bantam Doubleday Dell.

Naylor, P. R. (1991). *Shiloh*. New York: Dell Publishing.

Park, B. *Skinny-Bones*. (1997). New York: Random House.

Polacco, P. (1994). *Pink and Say*. New York: Scholastic.

_____. (1998). *Thank you, Mr. Falker*. New York: Philomel Books.

Prelutsky, J. & Smith, L. (1998). *Dr. Seuss: Hooray for diffendoofer day*. New York: Alfred Knopf.

Ray, K. W. (1999). *Wondrous words: Writers and writing in the elementary classroom*. Urbana, IL: National Council of Teachers of English.

Ringgold, F. (1993). *Dinner at Aunt Connie's house*. New York: Scholastic.

Rosenshine, B. (1997). Advances in research on instruction. In J. Lloyd, E. Kameenui, & D. Chard (Eds.) *Issues in educating students with disabilities* (pp. 197-220). Mahwah, NJ: Lawrence Erlbaum Associates.

Rylant, C. (1992). *Missing May*. New York: Bantm Doubleday Dell.

Shanahan, T., & Lomax, R. (1986). An analysis and comparison of theoretical models of the reading-writing relationship. *Journal of Educational Psychology*, 78, 116-123.

Simon, S. (1996). *The heart*. New York: Scholastic.

Spinelli, J. (1996). *Crash*. New York: Alfred A. Knopf.

Stone, A. (1998). Moving validated instructional practices into the classroom: Learning from examples about the rough road to success. *Learning Disabilities: Research and Practice* 13 (3), 121-125.

Swartz, R. & Parks, S. (1994). *Infusing the teaching of critical and creative thinking into content instruction*. Pacific Grove, CA: Critical Thinking Press & Software.

Taylor, M. D. (1990). *Mississippi bridge*. New York: Bantam Doubleday Dell.

Tsuchiya, Y. (1988). *Faithful elephants: A true story of animals, people and war*. Boston: Houghton Mifflin.

Wilkinson, L. (1995). Explicit teaching. In *Cornerstones: Training and developmental program. Adelaide, SA: Department of Education and Children's Services, Curriculum Division.*

Wilhelm, J. (2001). *Strategic reading: Guiding students to lifelong literacy 6-12*. Portsmouth, NH: Heinemann.

Williams, M. (1975). *The velveteen rabbit*. New York: Avon Books.

Williams, J.P. (1998). Improving comprehension of disabled readers. *Annals of Dyslexia*, 48, 213-238.

Yolen, J. (1993). *Welcome to the green house*. New York: Putnam & Grosset Group.

_____. (1996). *Welcome to the sea of sand*. New York: Penguin Putnam Books.

Index

About the Author

During her 25 years as a classroom teacher at different elementary grades, Dr. Nancy N. Boyles was named Teacher of the Year in her district and was a semi-finalist for Connecticut Teacher of the Year. She is presently the graduate reading program coordinator for Southern Connecticut State Univeristy where she teaches courses in developmental reading, content-area reading, writing instruction, and the administration of reading programs.

Dr. Boyles provides professional development to many school districts, presenting workshops, modeling Best Practice, and coaching teachers. Her areas of special interest include guided reading at the middle-grade level, expository writing, and building the skills of reading consultants.

Dr. Boyles has served as a contributing editor for *Learning Magazine* and has published over 30 articles related to teaching. She received her doctorate in reading and language from Boston University. She is the author of *Constructing Meaning Through Kid-Friendly Strategy Instruction* (Maupin House, 2004).